Contents

GEORGE HAYDUKE
MAKE `EM PAY!
Ultimate Revenge Techniques from the Master Trickster

Citadel Press / Secaucus, N.J.

5 4 3

Copyright © 1986 by Paladin Press
All rights reserved.
Published by Lyle Stuart Inc.
120 Enterprise Ave., Secaucus, N.J. 07094
In Canada: Musson Book Company
a division of General Publishing Co. Limited
Don Mills, Ontario
Manufactured in the United States of America
ISBN 0-8184-0421-3

Nelson Chunder Writes a Few Words About George Hayduke

My pal has been called the meanest man in the world and a true hyena in swine's clothing. Modest that he is, I know he cherishes both compliments. George always has been an affront to the pompous twits who rise to positions of power in our world. For instance, when George was born, the first peek of his personality shown to the world was his posterior.

I've known him since we were kids and I have fond memories of his mother's friends cowering in front of George's BB gun. I knew he'd be a contemporary author when his first literary masterpiece at the Norris Kindergarten was a four-letter word.

A few years later, George was returned from summer camp with a "Delivery Refused" tag on him. After he got out of school, the Army grabbed him and he quickly adopted two philosophies that have carried him far in his life. First, "in confusion there is profit." And second, he totally accepted General George S. Patton's belief that you don't win wars by dying for your country; you win wars by making the other poor bastard die for his country.

To complete the usual occupational trivia, let me report that George Hayduke has earned his keep as a laborer, minister, aircraft pilot, photographer, store detective, newspaper reporter, gun dealer, demolition man, public relations consultant, and now, as a full-time tosspot and Official Curmudgeon of the Ambrose Bierce Institute.

One of the finest testimonials Hayduke ever received came from the Bishop of Estonia and Idaho, the Right Holy Curtis Bevaqua, who said of George in a church pronouncement, *porcus ex grege diaboli* ("a swine from the devil's herd"). Tears of joyful acceptance from deep within George Washington Hayduke, Jr., flowed after that ringing endorsement.

I'm proud to be the friend of the meanest man in the world.

Introduction

"Can you see the Invisible Man's feces?"

I posed the question to my fellow philosophers as we sat around our table at the Gamboa Country Club in the bucolic village of Gamboa, Panama. It was January 1985 and my companions were Primo, El Presidente and Señor Tomas. Thinking that perversity makes for strange bedfellows, I repeated the question.

"It doesn't matter, my son," El Presidente said, as he sat deciding between a vigorous display of flatus and eructation, or, perhaps, a symphony of both. "You cannot capture the wind."

We savants of philosophy don't have much time left for our discussions or morality in a world gone mad. The Soviets and the Reaganistas are running throat to throat to see who can out-lie and out-bully the other to become master bully of the rest of the world. I was worrying a lot about my friends, the little folks. These are the powerless people who are the victims of bullies.

I liked the way Sid Bernstein, who's been writing a column in *Advertising Age* for years, puts it, *"It's not so much what you do that counts, but what you are willing to let the other fellow get away with."*

Aphoristically speaking, Sid is right. About 95 percent of the people are decent. They are ordinary citizens, straights and otherwise, who do not deliberately lie, steal, cheat or bully. They pay their taxes, try to hold jobs, are kind to other people and are good to their families. It's the 5 percent, though, who bully the 95 percent. I worry, too, because the moral indignation of the 95 percent seems to have atrophied in the past three or four years.

They get picked on, cheated, bullied and abused. And, as I've said, they just take it. Where is the fighting-back spirit? Where is the moral indignation that cries out, "I'm mad as hell and I'm not gonna take it anymore!" When do the 95 percent start to dish back the crap to the 5 percent?

Remember, you get walked on all over only when you throw yourself down in front of people!

For the few who have written to ask and for the most who haven't, I have been in Latin America much of the past two years involved in a variety of activities. During that time, Mac Chunder, a very close pal, has handled the book-writing chores and I want to thank him for a job well done. But for some months now, Mac has wanted to visit his ancestral home in the Australian outback. That, and the alarming plague of individual, corporate, institutional and governmental bullies at home, has hastened my return across our southern border.

I missed my country, my friends, my family and the little guys. It's time for an organized return to some entertainment by Haydukery.

The great author Chester Himes has a story that explains a great deal of the Hayduking philosophy without a lot of empty words. A friend of Mr. Himes, a man named Phil Lomax, told him about a pistol-toting blind guy who shot at a man who slapped him, but, accidentally killed an innocent bystander peacefully reading his newspaper.

I thought, damn right, sounds just like today's news, riots in the ghettos, war, masochistic doings in the Middle East. And then I thought of some of our loud-mouthed leaders urging our vulnerable soul brothers on to getting themselves killed, and thought further that all unorganized violence is like a blind man with a pistol.

Don't take that literally. In a sense it's a metaphor. I don't recall ever advocating that anyone be shot. Hell, every silver lining has its cloud, you know. I even reject the premise raised by some critics that my tactics are blunt and destructive. As the scholar and social scientist Abraham Maslow points out, "If the only tool you have is a hammer, you will treat everything like a nail."

To end this rhetorical meandering, I call on two people who probably would not share a page in the same book . . . unless it is my book. Though I despise much of his ideology and actions, I admire these words of Robert B. DePugh:

Our nation has reached a point of no return—a point beyond which the American people can no longer defend their freedom by the traditional means of politics and public opinion.

Finally, there is a man I wish were here to be our president today. I refer to Thomas Jefferson, who said in his first inaugural address in 1801:

Having banished from our land that religious intolerance under which mankind has so long bled and suffered, we have yet gained little if we countenance a political intolerance as despotic, as wicked, and capable of as bitter and bloody persecutions. . . . If there be any

5

among us who would wish to dissolve this Union or to change its republican form, let them stand undisturbed as monuments of the safety with which error of opinion may be tolerated, where reason is left free to combat it.

I thought about that beautiful sentiment from Mr. Jefferson as I read a final letter from a good friend in El Salvador who was born there and now must stay there forever. He wrote, "I do as you say, George. . . . do unto others, then split like hell."

Adios, amigo. Sometimes you get the eagle and sometimes the eagle gets you. Maybe this book can even some odds next time. When Talleyrand wrote, "There are two things to which we never grow accustomed—the ravages of time and the injustices of our fellow men," he was probably sure that we could attack only one of those dual assaults. That singularity is what this book is about.

—George W. Hayduke, Jr.
San Marcos, El Salvador
January 1986

How To Use This Book*

by M. Wellsley Spofford, Ph.D.

Mr. Hayduke asked me to write a foreword to his book, but I felt that too much pedagogical rhetoric would only cloud its definitive purpose, which is far beyond replication of his earlier philosophies. Instead, I opted to produce this methodological supplement for the reader's pragmatic edification.

As before, Mr. Hayduke has arranged his chapters both by subject and method, then arranged these alphabetically. In addition to searching chapter headings, he suggests you search other specific areas as many of the items lend themselves to more than one treatment. Indeed, in his classic review of Mr. Hayduke's original two books, Dr. Millard Plankton, the renowned professor of arcaneology at Louisiana School of Divinity, notes that some serious scholars of "Hayduking" have compiled extensive cross-indices of the various combinations of our author's classifications of marks/stunts/materials/methods, et cetera. Mr. Hayduke himself suggests that each reader perform an informal search or working cross-index of his or her own while using this book.

In the author's own words, "If you have a problem with some person or institution or whatever, look to the chapter heading of this book

---

*Reprinted from *Up Yours!* with the permission of Dr. Spofford.

for an appropriate response in solving your problem through the use of creative revenge. Look at some other headings, too, and you'll get more ideas to escalate your deserved revenge."

I can easily concur with that. Here, then, is Mr. Hayduke's newest book. Please, gentle reader, enjoy yourself.

Added Words of Wisdom From the Author

As my former mentor, Dr. Spofford, says, you can generate, then mix 'n match stunts in this book, just as in the earlier books by Mac Chunder and me. But nasty and personalized touches that are designed especially for your own mark make each hit more effective. Modification and customizing are grand ideas and I urge you to use them to match the crime and punishment. Remember that psychological warfare is almost always more devastating than the real thing. There's an old Creole belief that sums it up well, "Weso geye kofias na dlo, e se dlo ki kuit li," which means something like, "A fish trusts the water, and yet it is in the water that it is cooked."

GENERAL ADVICE

Throughout this book I will make universal reference to the "mark," which is a street label hung on the victim of a scam or con. In our case, the mark is anyone who has done something unpleasant, foul, unforgivable or fatal to you, your family, your property or your friends. Never think of a mark as the victim of dirty tricks. Think of the mark as a very deserving target of revenge.

Before you study any of the specific sections of this book, read these next few vital paragraphs. They tell you how to prepare before going into action.

1. Prepare a plan.

Plan all details before you take any action at all. Don't even ad-lib something from this book without a plan of exactly what you're going to do and how. If your campaign involves a series of actions, make a chronological chart, then coordinate your efforts. Make a list of possible problems. Plan what you'll do if you get caught—depending upon who catches you. You must have every option, contingency, action, reaction and evaluation planned in advance.

2. Gather intelligence.

Do what a real intelligence operative would do and compile a file on your mark. How detailed and thorough you are depends upon your plans for the mark. For a simple get-even number, you obviously need less intelligence than if you're planning an involved, time-release campaign. Before you start spying, make a written list of all the important things you need to know about the target—be it a person, company or institution.

3. Buy away from home.

Any supplies, materials or services you need must be purchased away from where you live. Buy way in advance and pay in cash. Try to be as inconspicuous and colorless as possible. Don't talk unnecessarily with people. The best rule here is the spy's favorite—a good agent will get lost in a crowd of one. The idea is for people not to remember you.

4. Never tip your hand.

Don't get cocky, cute 'n clever and start dropping hints about who's doing what to whom. I know that may sound stupid, but some would-be tricksters are gabby. Of course, in some of the cases this will not apply, e.g., unselling car customers at the dealership, or other tricks in which the scenario demands your personal involvement.

5. Never admit anything.

If accused, act shocked, hurt, outraged or amused, whichever seems most appropriate. Deny everything, unless, again, your plan involves overt personal involvement. If you're working covert, stay that way. The only cool guy out of Watergate was Gordon Liddy; he kept his mouth shut.

6. Never apologize; it's a sign of weakness.

Normally, harassment of a citizen is a low-priority case with the police. The priority increases along with the person's socio-financial position in the community and with his or her political connections. If you are at war with a corporation, utility or institution, that's a different ball game. They often have private security people, sometimes retired federal or state investigators. By habit, these people may not play according to the law. If you play dirty tricks upon a governmental body be prepared to have a case opened. But how hard it is followed depends upon a lot of factors. Understanding all this ahead of time is part of your intelligence planning before you get started in action.

Caution

The schemes, tricks, scams, stunts, cons, and scenarios presented here are solely for information and amusement purposes only. It is not my intent that you use this book as a manual or trickster's cookbook. I certainly don't expect that anyone who reads this book would actually ever *do* any of the things described here.

This book is written to entertain and inform readers, not to instruct or persuade them to commit any illegal act. From my own mild disposition, I could hardly tell someone else to make any of these tactics operational.

Consider the case of mistaken vengeance that took place in Vienna, Austria, in 1985, when Leopold Renner thought his wife was cheating on him because he saw her holding hands with another man. The shocked husband stuffed twenty-seven of her live, exotic pets—one after another—into the churning garbage disposal. Down went screaming parakeets, hamsters, mice and tarsiers into a gushy gruel feeding into the sewage drains.

Fact: His wife Frieda was holding the hand of her brother, whom she had not seen in a dozen years, and was bringing him home to meet her husband. True story.

Please read this book with that reference in mind. Remember, it's all in good clean fun, isn't it? That was a rhetorical question.

Airlines

Here's a wonderful variation on one of the old airline message jokes. It came about because Geneth of Houston was tired of flight delays and hassles, all excused by lies about airport security. An idea formed in Geneth's mind.

The primary mark was the least favorite airline. A secondary mark was a passenger chosen in the terminal because of some form of rude on-site or other crude behavior. The medium was a handwritten note done by one friend, while the delivery system was another friend of Geneth's who left the airport immediately after handing the note in a sealed envelope to a boarding attendant at the gate, along with this verbal request:

"See that man/woman ahead, just getting on? That's my uncle/aunt (husband/wife, son/daughter, etc.) and I have a nice birthday surprise (smile a whole lot) for him/her. Would you please give him/her this note when you get airborne? It's OK if everyone wants to sing along. Gee, (laugh), is old (name) going to be surprised."

The note that will be opened in-flight by an unsuspecting mark contains one of these three messages:

1. Please be discreet. If you have any flying experience come to the front of the airplane; the pilot's dead.
2. This airplane has been hijacked and the terrorists have chosen you to be dumped out

of the cargo hatch as a symbol. Come to the cockpit or we'll blow up the airplane.

3. A four-year old girl/boy has identified you as the person who molested him/her in the bathroom of the airport just before departure. We are holding you for arrest until landing in _____ .

This will create some fun, and some confusion. It will work best if neither of the marks, primary or secondary, has a sense of humor.

If you are a frequent flier, you will note how the human cattle called passengers line up at the restrooms shortly after the in-flight meal has assaulted their systems. You might beat the line next time you're aloft and put a generous coating of Elmer's glue on both the top and bottom of the toilet seat while the meal is being served.

Animals

For a lot of real and symbolic reasons, animals have always been great tools of revenge, going back to our fears of our evolutionary ancestors, I suppose. Using animals in your stunts will definitely put you ahead of the others in the revenge business.

In some areas you can buy dog and cat inmates from the pound for as little as a buck or two apiece. Buy a bunch of these condemned prisoners and hold them as your guests until . . .

You've been fired or insulted by the idiot boss of a bar or restaurant, or you got a lousy meal there. Maybe you hate the owner for what he or she did to your family. There could be a dozen reasons for what you're about to do.

Take your menagerie of four-footed friends to every available door of the marked location and get them all as far inside as possible. You may wish to disguise yourself and your drivers. After your herd is safely delivered, you should depart. Bedlam is a modest word to describe what will happen next, especially if your furry dinner guests are really, truly hungry. Condition them that way before delivery, of course.

Own a live trap, one of those Havahart numbers? Great. Catch a wild raccoon, opossum, groundhog or feral cat in it. Turn this animal loose in your mark's car or apartment. Think about the state of that environment after half an hour of attempted escape, followed by frantic trashing.

Answering Machines

Maybe it's because he's from Oakland and had to put up with Al Davis all those years, but Chester the Spoon has some advice for folks who don't like answering machines. He suggests you make many, many repeated calls over a thirty- or forty-minute period and leave either no message or rude, untraceable ones. The idea is to overload the machine and, perhaps, make the mark miss an important call.

A more direct method, which comes from Alik Allotjka, requires access to your mark's answering machine, which, of course, would be easy in a business office. But don't forget social occasions when you might have a free run of his or her home. It's a great way to pay back someone who's used a telephone to abuse you in one form or another. Prerecord an answering-machine message of your own design in your mark's name. Make it awful, crude or whatever would do the most damage. Substitute this tape for the one already in the machine. Do it during a time period when you know it will get maximum play.

Anti-Abortionists

The wife of one of my friends had a completely unrelated business meeting in the same building that housed an abortion clinic. As she tried to enter the lobby, she was attacked by a gaggle of right-to-life harridans. This quiet, small lady, who was a computer consultant going to a job with a financial office on another floor of the large building, was almost in a panic.

"They screamed at me, called me a murderer, pushed me. Then one of them spit right in my face. They were some local group from the neighborhood Catholic Church. I was too scared to be shocked," she recalled, almost in tears, nearly a month later.

Furious, her husband went to the police and was told that nothing could be done without independent witnesses. He was also told, off the record, that the police chief and the priest at the church were bosom buddies and the police were told to lean on the clinic and leave the pickets alone. Frustrated, he came to me.

The statute of limitations of the state involved make it impossible for me to relate precisely what was done to 1) the picketing group's leaders, 2) that local Catholic Church, 3) its priest, and, 4) the local police chief. Be assured, it was appropriate and heavy duty. Maybe a volume or two from now I can tell you all about the repayment for their uncivilized behavior.

In any case, if you happen to believe in a woman's freedom to make her own choices about her own life and body and reject the ravings of the harpies who think otherwise, simply pick and choose from almost any of the stunts in this and the other revenge books, adapt it to your needs, and go from there. I would also very much like to hear from those of you out there who have had similar run-ins.

Armed Forces

Is there any low life enlisted man who has not faced the anger, if not the rotted breath, of a hung-over sergeant with gusto but no justice in his soul? Allen Watkins told me about one of his friends who tired of being the object of a scapegoat routine of a drunken lout of a leader. He opened the hood of the NCO's car while he had CQ duty one night and packed some tear gas into the intake manifold of the vehicle's air-conditioning unit.

Oh, did I mention that our hero was clearing post the next day? Some weeks later a friend's letter explained the humorous news that the NCO spent two days in the base hospital.

Having been an Army grunt, I have never seen an aircraft carrier except in films or at a great distance. My old pal, a Navy vet named Gino the Engine King Chemist, tells me they are massive.

I'm not sure how he knows as he was in submarines, except for the time he had a gaggle of Italian whores chase him through town for not paying his tab at the Eat 'n Hump. Anyway, Nanker Phelge, another Navy man, says that some carriers show films or have live Bob Hope-type shows in the enclosed hangar decks.

"Do you have any idea how much volume of water is carried in the fire control/sprinkler system of these ships?"

His question was more than rhetorical as I had no idea, not even knowing the Navy had sprinkler systems. He told me it was more a deluge system than a sprinkler. He refused to be specific as he still has a rating in our Imperial Emperor's U.S. Navy, but he says some guys with a grudge against someone got high enough to build a strong and very hot heat source under the fire-control sensors on the hangar roof. They used propane torches. Within five minutes, the hangar was flooded. The evening's show was a washout in the true sense of the word.

As a vet, I always liked Senator Joe Clark's pungent observation that a leader should not get too far in front of his troops or "he might get shot in the ass." On the other hand, I wondered about that when I read the graffiti that Edward Gein had written in the main restroom of the Bates Motel: "The alternative to getting old is depressing."

Associations

Deciding who is the worst among current totalitarian leaders is like deciding from which bucket of buzzard puke to drink. For starters, here is some help with an easier choice—making life bad for some true jerks. The best part is that you can use people's natural inclination to "join" as your ally.

It happens. Some group like Gay Awareness, or Coal Companies to Desecrate America, or Veterans to Invade the Pentagon does something heinous to you. Compounding this latest affront is your mark—a neighbor, boss, coworker or some other fool—whom you have placed on the association's roster without his or her knowledge. If you like the ideas that follow, thank Bartholomew McGillicudy.

"Advertise your mark's home or apartment as the meeting place for the nasty group," advises Bart. "Use different media to advertise—public service spots on local radio and TV, newspaper mentions, ads, notices in stores. Hit all the local outlets. Tell people in bars and grocery stores."

As an extra suggestion, you can also get hold of the floating mike at the local department store or entire mall complex and sneak in an announcement or two. Keep 'em brief, like ten seconds, and then split as soon as you're off the air.

At the suggestion of Don Lucely, here are some dummy organizations you can sponsor:
• Herpes Without Partners

- AIDS Where It Hurts
- Gay Rights Sleep-in
- Proud to Be Pederast Parents
- Chlamydia Victims Cookout
- Immoral Mothers of _____ County

Attitude

While I was working as an agricultural consultant in Latin America recently, I found a wonderful story that would make Norman Vincent Peale's wellsprings of humanity overflow. The lady in this story has the best possible attitude for coping with being either Hayduker or Haydukee.

This American tourist Yuppie lady awoke in her Cancun condo way beyond her normal 7 a.m. Nautilus time and was feeling very fierce. She groaned a few times, whined about drinking too much wine cooler, then realized that there was something wrong with her hair.

She stuck her fashionably thin hand up there, felt around and found a couple dozen grains of rice scattered throughout her coiffeur. Trying to recall the latter part of the evening, she thought and thought.

Giving up with a pained look of resignation, she whined, "Well, either I got married again last night or I was puked on by a Chinaman."

Auto Dealers

The Skull really does have a sense of fair humor when he deals with these purveyors of generally putrid products. As before, he had another run-in with a car dealer who screwed him on a badly misrepresented vehicle. After the usual honest and open attempts to right this wrong, Skull thought of other ways.

He set up a lemon stand in a public area outside the dealership after taking out the necessary "street merchant" license to peddle the fruit. It cost five dollars. He made a large sign that read: WHY PAY THOUSANDS FOR A LEMON ACROSS THE STREET? In smaller type, it read: I'LL GIVE YOU A FREE LEMON.

And, Skull did . . . passing out dozens of lemons to bemused would-be customers of the dealer. Some tossed their lemons at the salesmen standing outside the dealership trying to wish away Skull's legal form of Haydukery.

"After an hour and a half nobody had gone into the dealership" reports Skull. "The service manager came over and tried to provoke a fight. A friend of mine, who had been preprimed, called the police and the local TV stations. We got a lot more coverage than I even planned."

Skull says that the very same evening the dealership's manager got in touch with him and agreed to make right the previous screwing-over our hero had gotten on his car deal.

Autos

You remember Alex Foley, the Detroit cop, who suggested good ideas for bad guys? Here's a sample of his fun for their rides: a banana in the tail pipe has the same effect as the Hayduke potato but it's a lot less dangerous for the person standing behind the car.

I can't vouch for this, but if old Shadow says it works, it does. He has been around. But, let's say your mark has a car you don't like either. According to Shadow, you take a Spaulding Ping Pong ball—he says it has to be a Spaulding because of the chemical makeup—fill it with liquid drain cleaner, using a hypodermic needle, then wrap black electrical tape all around.

"Drop that sucker in the vehicle's gas tank and it will stand that car *on its nose,*" says Shadow. "You can experiment with the amount of tape you use according to how much time you need to get away . . . the more tape there is, the longer it takes for the gas to eat through."

Next is a hotshot in the dark from Shadow. Use some crazy-type glue to adhere a shotgun shell to a hot part of your mark's auto or bike engine. As a humanitarian, Shadow suggests that (1) you don't work on an engine part that is hot, and (2) it would be nice to remove the shot load from the shell first, but leave the wadding in place.

Shep from Denver has a dilly way to get even with a car tinkerer who's done him some dirt. Shep says, "Just put a half dozen of those baby dills in his gas-tank outlet. When that engine kicks over and runs, the fuel pump will suck those little dills right up into the gas line."

He adds that when he was once busted totally without reason in Kansas City, he retaliated by pulling this stunt on more than a few of the vehicles in the police department's official automobile pool. Expensive mechanical chaos was their repayment bill for his unjustified bust.

It was good to hear from the Yakima Rt. 1 Auto Flush and his wife as they share some fun for your mark's auto. First, they suggest removing a couple spark plugs, dropping a few small ball bearings into the cylinders, and then replacing the plugs. The results are expensive to repair, in the neighborhood of $400 to $500 for labor alone.

Their next idea will work wonderfully if the mark bought his or her car from an out-of-town dealer. When the mark is at work and the car is parked in a non-patrolled zone, call a tow service and explain there are problems with "your" car. You must be "Mr. Mark/Owner" during this call, of course.

Have the car towed to the local dealership—hopefully on a Friday afternoon—and tell them you're going away for the weekend and will get back to them Monday or Tuesday. As most dealers are slow, this vehicle could sit for a week before someone—the real owner and the police—start to get seriously worried about it.

Does your mark have a vehicle with an automatic transmission? Most do these days, as many marks are real wimps—prime market for the autoshifters. Our Yakima mechanic says the solution is simple: pour a quart of battery acid in with the transmission fluid. Soon, no transmission.

Several mechanics from the Pinkeln Auto Repair School suggested that you have a friendly

26

mechanic reverse the sensor between the gas gauge and the gas tank of your mark's car. This will be a lot of fun for your mark some dark, stormy night miles from nowhere.

Mark Hastings lives in a neighborhood full of stuffed shirts and materialistic, bragging Yuppies. He finally had some fun with the vehicle of one from this breed of jerks. The air pressure in the new metric radial tires is fairly critical. Mark adjusted the air pressure in the mark's car tire over a two-week period and had the snobbish Yuppie running the soles off his Nikes in frustration.

"I increased pressure in the right front to sixty pounds one night. Two nights later, I decreased that one to twenty pounds and increased the left front to sixty," Mark says.

Mark was able to learn when this Yuppie was taking his car into the dealership to check the front-end "handling" problems, and the night before he normalized the pressure.

"The dumb jerk spent about $200 on new parts and repair time, plus the dealer's mechanics just kept putting new things on his car. It was great fun hassling this fool," relates Mark.

We need more folks like Jennifer Marshall. Her mind is magnificently malevolent. But, alas, she's on her own out there doing rotten things to evil people as just another avenging angel.

Here is her latest. There are gasoline additives that rid a car's engine of excess moisture. That is, unless you use three bottles on your mark's car. That dosage will heat the average auto-engine temperature beyond not only belief, but also beyond workable stress. Hello, big repair bills.

And, from the fun world of doing radio talk shows, I learned from Denver Don that you can sour an auto battery into inaction by filling it with vinegar. Also, if you fill an auto's gas tank with aircraft fuel, it will not be a happy experience for the vehicle, its owner, or the folks standing nearby when the owner tries to start 'er up.

Can you believe that some guy by the name of Dick Smegma, who claims the title of international revenge master, thinks that the stunts Nelson Chunder and I report to you are tame? Perhaps, though, Dick's right. For example, he suggests pouring crystallized drain cleaner into the gas tank of your mark's car.

"Want a demonstration?" Dick asks rhetorically. "Try one grain of the stuff in a teaspoon of gasoline before you move to anything operational."

I did. It creates quite a reaction. This is an unsafe trick without grand planning. Use a slow delivery system with insulation or learn to run faster than an explosion you don't want to be caught in.

Dick's stuff is fairly explicit, so you'll be reading a great deal more about him as you peruse this book.

Remember "Send a Boy to Camp?" Let's buy a car for your mark, or, at least in your mark's name. It may cost you $25 holding money or maybe a few bucks more. But, you can do it. Fill out all the forms and if you've played the salesperson just right and he or she is hungry, you will get away with it. Money speaks louder than ID. Obviously, you must know your mark's name, address and all that so you can fill in the binding legal forms. Pay cash for your small down payment, then leave. Or, see if the salesperson will let you drive the car to the bank to get your loan money. You promise to drive right back. Park the car somewhere irregular and leave town with a friend. This probably works best with a used car and a hungry dealer. The legal hassle for the mark remains the same.

Bad Checks

You've been had by a friend who likes to fly bad checks. Moral persuasion doesn't turn red ink to black and friendship refuses to balance things. It's time to kick-start the tongues of the local gossip brigade. The Baffling Radiologist suggests that you post all of your "friend's" bad debts and credit risks on public location bulletin boards, especially at neighborhood groceries, super-markets and malls. You can also post the culprit's name on the lists of bad-check writers that a lot of businesses carry on their registers and checkout counters in full view of the public.

BB Machine Guns

For the dozen or so folks who've written to ask about LARC's neat BB guns, it sells two models: an M19A, which is a little submachine gun, and the big model, which is a machine gun. Both fire BBs using compressed air. Both shoot a hell of a lot of BBs in a short time. LARC is located at 736 Industry Road, Longwood, FL 32750.

Beds

Remember that wonderful scene in *M*A*S*H* when the guys wired for full audio the bunk being used by Hotlips and Frank for fornication purposes? Any competent bugger could do this, either for live broadcast or to be taped for later use, say at a school assembly, dance, wedding celebration, graduation, job interview, etc. See "Sources" for both instructions and equipment.

Body Parts

I'm not sure if Ray came up with this one or not. We were all fairly drunk down in Cabo San Lucas when the idea came up. Anyway, if your mark has a morbid fear of death and pieces of dead things, and most marks do or they wouldn't qualify as marks, you might beg, borrow or steal human body parts from the nearest physiology or anatomy laboratory. Send these to your mark. You can customize or personalize this in any way you wish. What the hell, it's a step up the evolutionary ladder from roadkill.

Bombs

It's not especially enlightening, but you could set off a road flare or a smoke bomb in your mark's home. The flares are easier to deal with than smoke bombs, now sold openly to aid folks lost in big forests, which cause more hassle. Can you imagine your mark coping with 50,000 cubic feet of white, blue or red smoke billowing around his or her domicile?

Because of cost factors, the Provos in Ulster switched from conventional explosives to chemical bombs a few years ago. Components for these beasties are easily available in rural and farming areas where agricultural supply stores abound. In simple form, sugar added to sodium chlorate or sodium nitrate, along with nitrobenzene or diesel fuel as a catalyst, makes a generic chemical bomb. Of course, these substances together are as highly unstable as those who use them in Ireland.

Anyway, there are many books available telling you how to convert handy backyard garden products into enough explosives to demolish your mark's chicken coop, outhouse or stash. Personally—well, no, I promised I wouldn't moralize in this volume.

According to a fan who tells me he is a former state legislator from New England, one of the finer bombs ready for funny use is a television picture tube from one of the older, ten years or more, abandoned sets. They blow up loudly.

"If your mark has wronged you with his car, place one of these tubes under his car frame where you know movement will crush it. When the mark moves the car, the tube will explode with a hell of a blast and send glass flying every which way. It might even cut some hoses on the car," our fan exclaims with glee.

My God, an honest, used politician with some sense, including one of humor. No wonder he's an ex.

Books

Our same reformed politician from New Hampshire wishes to share some literary fun. If you have any marks who can read, provide them with free bookmarks. Our contributor suggests very thin slices of cheese or cold cuts (salami is great) between the pages. This will work well for the mark who has shelves of unread books just for the ego-image they afford him.

In addition to their use as weapons themselves, books contain lots of ammunition to be fired at your marks. What follows is a collection of books with themes, ideas and thoughts to help the neophyte Hayduker. These books are especially good friends:

Hoffman, E. J. *Nitration of Toluene*. Bradley, IL: Lindsay Publications, 1984.
> Want to make your own TNT? This reprint of a turn-of-the-century manual from the U.S. Bureau of Mines gives you a step-by-step cookbook to adding nitric acid to toluene.

Horvitz, Simeon L. *Legal Protection for Today's Consumer*. Dubuque, IA: Kendall Hunt, 1981.
> A grand workbook, an inspirational tome for folks interested in effectively using consumer protection legislation and available myriad legal remedies.

Kneitel, Tom. *Top Secret Registry of U.S. Government Radio Frequencies.* Commack, NY: CRB Research, 1985.

Peterson, Bozo and Hendrick, J. G. *The Roadkill Cookery Book.* Phoenix: Hilliard-Townsend First Mate Press, 1985.

Tayacan (pseudo). *Psychological Operations in Guerrilla Warfare.* Washington: Central Intelligence Agency, 1984.
Despite being the Company's famed assassination how-to boo-boo of the '80s, this nifty number has some other mind-fornicating tricks in it that can be adapted by a creative Hayduker. See your tax dollars at work for you.

Thomas, Ralph D. *Physical Surveillance Manual.* Boulder: Paladin Press, 1984.
This is an excellent handbook by a very professional private investigator. He gives detailed instructions on gathering a lot of information on any subject, aka, your mark.

Weingart, George. *Pyrotechnics.* Bradley, IL: Lindsay Publications, 1984.
Making your own fireworks for use against your enemies can be fun and probably safer than trying to smuggle them. This is a reprint of a rare 1947 "how-to" book that tells and shows you how to make all sorts of fun things.

Worthen, K. J. *Preserving the Dead: The Art and Science of Embalming.* Bradley, IL: Lindsay Publications, 1984.
This is a reprint of a fairly grotesque and tacky book. The content aside, I can see some delightful uses for the art and science described herein. It might also make a thoughtful gift for someone you hate.

Bucket
Above the Door

Who else but Dick Smegma would have the intestinal fortitude to update this hoary old cliché Dick suggests filling the old water bucket with something more modern than water. His list includes liquid skunk smell, hydrochloric acid, horse urine or urined-down excrement. Dick says placement is crucial. I add that disguising the smell, unless you're dealing with a drunk, allergy or head-cold victim, is also vital.

Bumper Stickers

My buddy, the Hombre for Justice, first wrote me a sad letter telling me how he was an unaggressive sort of guy who was always being picked upon and bullied, and how he hated himself. He read a couple of my books, plus suffered more nastiness by uncaring institutions and people, then finally crossed over to being a person who gets back at his tormentors. It is an inspirational story that brings lumps to my eyes and tears to my throat.

Hombre likes to use bumper stickers and gets his printed salvation from the various companies (see "Sources") that sell custom stickers. Here is a partial inventory of the bumper stickers that Hombre uses on his mark's cars, buildings, offices, homes, etc.

- SCREW LAZY AMERICANS, DRIVE A FOREIGN CAR
- GOD SUCKS
- GOD SUCKS AND GIVES CHANGE
- I ♥ COMMUNISM
- HAVE YOU HIT YOUR KID TODAY?
- (Team Name) FANS ARE PUSSIES
- BIKERS ON HARLEYS ARE QUEER
- I'M MARRIED TOO, LET'S SCREW
- FOR FREE SEX CALL (include mark's number)
- HONK IF YOU WANT HEAD

Dick Smegma is a professional nastyman.

Check out the big league style he has for the use of bumper stickers. First, Dick says they should never be placed on a mark's bumper. "Always place them on the trunk lids and smooth them down tight. Use the 'super-stick' kind that remove the paint when they come off."

Finally, thanks to Shadow for a couple more sticker ideas:

- I'M PROUD TO HAVE HERPES
- AID ME TO GET MORE AIDS
- I ♥ AIDS
- HERPES/AIDS, PASS IT ON

Campers

Does it ever boil your temper over into the red area on a hot summer's day when some camper stays in the communal comfort station (aka public crapper) for twenty or thirty minutes reading the newspaper? A fan by the name of Wolfgang Creutzfeldt is only kidding around, of course, with his solution to this irritating face flusher.

"Get a tin can and fill it half full of Koolaid—the drink for kids. Then, set it inside the outside door of the crapper. Take a red-hot coal from a nearby camp fire and drop it into the Koolaid. Instant smoke! Lots of it," claims Creutzfeldt. "You can experiment with other additives to mix in with the Koolaid. I've tried hot chili sauce with screaming success. It makes a lot of truly obnoxious smoke."

Candy

My fellow author, Barney Vincelette, edited this shaggy dog tale into a short, sweet stunt. Barney says to get some blood-inflated ticks and chocolate-coat them. Let them ripen a week. Serve them to your mark. They burst in the mark's mouth, not in your hand.

Bothersome Burt is happy to be a rotten egg during the Easter holiday season as he points out that candy eggs make a nice mark target. He says to slice off the top of the candy egg, leaving it still encased in the foil. Remove the sweet contents of the candy egg and replace with any sort of vile concoction. Burt says not to use liquids, though, as they leak. The imagination almost goes into overload, however, thinking of all the disgusting solids and mushy things you can plant in there before you close it back up and gently melt the chocolate seam together again. Then squeeze the foil shut and serve.

Charlatans

Now, for some comedic relief, brought to you by Lil Eddie Meese. Remember our "Nobody's hungry, cold, in poverty, or hurting in the USA," attorney general? Remember him? Here's a fun little game you can play with other fascist friends.

1. Print Ronald Reagan's full name (all three of 'em) on a paper.
2. Count the number of letters in each name.
3. Place that number above the respective name.
4. Write the three numbers together, side by side.
5. Mail the completed paper to Jerry Falwell.

This one makes them froth at the mouth every time.

Chemicals

Here's something from my politician friend from New Hampshire. He says that hydrogen sulfide (H_2S) is the gas that gives rotten eggs their wonderful odor. High school chemistry classes use this gas for research. You can obtain small, open-ended glass vials of a compound that when heated produces volumes of H_2S. While these vials are supposed to be used in chemistry experiments, you could use them to experiment on your mark's automobile manifold, wood stove, radiator or some other spot in which heat is generated. Get the vials from a chemical supply shop.

The ingredients in crystallized drain cleaner are very versatile (See "Auto" section). You can also toss an open can of this product into the mark's swimming pool—if it contains water. Dumping a canful into a washer during the final rinse is spectacular, too.

Remember our old friend ipecac from my first book? It can also be self-administered if you want to make a mark's restaurant, for example, very nervous about your illness. Here's how it works. Eat a colorful portion of your meal. Go into the restroom and swallow the contents of a very small container (one ounce or less) of a vomit-inducer that contains ipecac. Cut the plastic bottle up into pieces and flush them down the commode. Flush twice more to be sure. Go back out and resume your meal. In about ten minutes you will be wracked by projectile vomiting. Be creative and use all your acting ability here to get maximum splatter and mass audience effect.

According to a pamphlet distributed by the International Brotherhood of Barfing Engineers, a good way to do this is "to move erratically and quickly among the other diners as you appear to be headed toward the bathroom. Your real objective, of course, is to strafe as many people as possible with your vomitus."

This is a grand way to mess up someone's home or get back at a restaurant or other mark that has made you literally ill in one form or another. Advice: Try a dry run (no pun) first so you see how you can handle this self-administered ipecac attack. Normally, the real thing is over in about five minutes and you'll have no aftereffects. Now, let's move on from puking to planting, or, rather, unplanting.

Even though your local K-Mart sells OK weedkillers and other commercial herbicides, you can get even better and more efficient vegetation wasters at farm supply stores. A fine gentleman known as the King of Lexington offers the advice that many splendid plant-killing chemicals are available there. Being an old farm boy, he'd know.

"An example of an easily available and safe herbicide is Monsanto's Round-Up which can be aerially applied to a mark's lawn or garden by water balloon, or you can use a sprayer to write nasty words or whole messages if you have the space," our monarch notes.

Meanwhile, moving to the fabric section, it's nice to learn that methyl violet will permanently stain clothing. A little of it in any laundry soap will go a long way in ruining your mark's wardrobe. According to Tanya of Long Beach, a box of Rit or Tintex dye will work also. This is a grand idea for apartment laundry rooms where your mark is a regular.

CIA

As old Papa Doc from Haiti used to say before being bumped and dumped by the CIA, "Only the knife knows what's in the heart of the yam." Obviously, our government does have a sense of humor. How else can you explain the operations of the Central Intelligence Agency?

A good friend of mine is a reporter for National News Service and he brought me back from Honduras one of the very first "exported" copies of that secret CIA assassination manual (see "Books"). Yup, this was long before the Washington Press Corps discovered it and thus made it real.

Anyway, if you think the CIA doesn't have a sense of humor, you should see the early issue of "CIA Comix," their infamous illustrated manual for mayhem and murder that was given to Contra terrorists down there to show them how to do illegal things to the legally elected government of Nicaragua.

Happily, my Spanish language literary level is at least on a par with the Contras so I was able to read this comic book that you and I overpaid some CIA consultant to plagiarize, write, illustrate, print and distribute. It contains a lot of interesting stunts that you could adopt for your own use. For starters, report late for work, then slough off the rest of the day. Clog toilets in your office and other buildings. Leave water running. Damage expensive office equipment. Make fake airline and hotel reservations. Call in false fire and police alarms. Cut telephone lines. Spray-paint anti-government slogans. Waste public officials. On the last one, the CIA insisted it did not mean to murder them. Bull. Most public officials are a waste anyway so what's it matter, as one of my old CIA chums once said.

Order your copy now. Write the publisher, the CIA, and be the first kid on your block to topple someone's infrastructure, or to start an insurrection. If the CIA is out of copies, check with some of the commercial publishers who did rip-off versions.

Communism

With the second coming of the Reaganistas, the old bogey word "communism" has been dug up again to scare anyone who doesn't march along with the other mindless cattle in Cowboy Ronny's herd of unthinking Americans. That's why Chris Schaefer has a grand idea to take advantage of this unnatural, national paranoia.

Get a copy of official letterhead from the USSR, Cuba or one of the Soviet's Middle East satellite countries. That's easy enough, just write to their government with some inane question that needs only a routine reply. Take their letterhead logo either to your printer or to a copy machine to make new, blank letterhead. Now, type some sort of cryptic, code-appearing messages on it . . . like "The red fish sails" or "Bach comes alive in thirty days," or some silliness like that. Mail this letter to your mark who works for a large defense contractor or one of the sensitive government agencies.

Hope that the secretary will open the mail first—this is usually the case. With luck she will show it to the mark's superior or to security people.

Computers

Eons ago, it seems, I told you about the advent of X-rated computer games. Now, Bothersome Burt refines this trend. He knew a guy in school who used to cheat on computer assignments by using other people's programs. Burt decided to share, too.

"Make a copy of one of those 'dirty old men' X-rated game disks, making sure it has really obscene graphics. Label it with the mark's name and the identification of some popular program, then put it in the school's computer room library. Red faces in the sunset," Burt says with a chortle.

Condoms

If you're a spouse of a mark who is always unfaithful, here's an idea. Send him or her a condom filled with mayonnaise and include this note: "You forgot this souvenir last night." Even if you are the other party involved, you can do the same thing.

Convenience Stores

There has been a disturbing trend across the U.S. where local right-think Bible thumpers are blackmailing convenience store management into banning harmless magazines from their shelves. For instance, in the East, the Sheetz chain of quickie stops banned such horrible publications as *Playboy* because a group of religious loonies threatened to boycott them. In other parts of the country, 7/11 stores fell to the same pressure from these mindless slimeballs.

Enough idiotorializing (editorials about idiots), let's do something. For that, I call on our dynamic duo, Filthy McNasty and his fine friend Vera, for their help. Here's their plan.

Locate the most disgusting pictures you can find. Use your imagination to locate something that will disgust everyone, even farm animals. Reproduce this photograph on the type of advertising flyer that stores put under windshield wipers of cars parked in large shopping malls. Along with the photo, put some advertising slogan like "You can't beat our meat," or "Get your rocks off here," or, "If you think this looks like fun, ask our clerk about the daily special." Then, include in large type the name of the store you want to Hayduke.

Don't feel sorry for the store. These gutless wimps surrendered to our enemy in the battle for freedom. Freedom of our minds is far too valuable to surrender to some evil bluenose wearing his hypocritical God-squad mask.

Cookouts

As noted earlier, Mark Hastings is a prisoner in Yuppieland. Happily, he has discovered another way of doing guerrilla warfare against his captives.

"I found that soaking charcoal briquettes in transmission fluid and then replacing them in Mr. Yuppie's bag is spectacular fun. He soaks them in lighter fluid and lights them up. You would not believe the smoke. All the Yuppies wimp off inside to get away from that horrible lung pollution."

Corrections

A number of loyalists wrote to correct M. Chunder's error in *Mad as Hell* over hookahs and bongs. We both apologize, although I don't know why I am, as it was his stupid error, not mine. Anyway, neither of us are dopers. In fact, he thought hookahs were New England prostitutes and I thought a bong was something from the start of a J. Arthur Rank Organization film. Sigh.

We stand corrected now, so stop sending us all the free samples. What will we do with them all?

Customs Service

If your mark has been or will travel out of the country, you might want to help make a memorable return home by filling out a U.S. customs declaration in his/her/their name. Forms may be obtained at international airports. After being creatively completed, it can be left in an airport, smuggled into a customs area or given to airport security. It would all depend how and upon whom you chose to use it.

Dead Animals

Thanks and a tip of the Hayduke halo to Tim W. Newton for this charming use for previously live animals. Tim used to use full-size roadkill for Haydukery, then he got into the idea of nerve terror after reading M. Chunder's last book.

"The idea is to make the mark think some cult or loony is paying attention to him or her," Tim says with glee. "What I do is get very small dead animals and birds, like chipmunks, baby bunnies, or sparrows. I nail them to a cross or board. Sometimes I paint funny designs on them or on the board. I always try to include a photo of the mark and/or his family which I've taken with a long telephoto lens."

That, I imagine, could just shake the effluvia out of anyone.

You remember Carla Savage. She says that roadkill and other dead animals are like cops, they're never around when you need one. But, since moving to California, she has found a remedy to this shortage of dead animals.

"Being in the horse business, I know a lot of people with big old barns. Big old barns have rats. They also have rat traps, poison and ill-paid illegals from Mexico to dispose of the rodents.

"I give the Mexicans a bunch of baggies each week, then pay them twenty-five cents per rat, more if the rat is really big and gross," Carla writes. "When I told them what I planned to do, they were thrilled at my getting back at some rich creep, so they began to volunteer things for my collection of putrescent carcasses—dead lizards, jack rabbits, snakes, and something so large and foul that even Chief Medical Examiner Quincy couldn't identify it."

Carla's little zoo soon began to appear in the swimming pool, tennis court and, eventually, the water well of her neighbor, a man who had given her and her own live animals mega-reasons for revenge.

Death Pool

The credit for this fine bit of American ingenuity goes to Barb, Ray and Tom. With some modification you can make it work on your mark. You send a memo or call your mark on the telephone. Ask if he/she wants in on "The Death Pool." Explain that the player coming the closest to the actual death date of the subject in the next six months wins the pool. When asked the inevitable "Who is going to die?" question, you reply calmly, "We've picked you."

As a visual aide, you might create a Death Pool calendar with the choices listed. Display it in a high-traffic location in the office, dorm, barracks or whatever.

Diplomas

You know the insecure, sissy kids who sort of grew up to be wimps today? These are the folks who hide their lack of talent, skills, security, balls, brains, beauty, common sense, humanism, humorlessness, etc., behind job title, degrees, rank, position or marriage. One of their telltale spoor is the glass-framed credential, usually in the office or open-to-guests area of the home.

Chester the Spoon says, "Use permanent markers to make big slashes across their credential security shields."

Dog Waste

Bill Overton of Granite City, IL, was not fond of his neighbor's canines because of their annoying habit of loud, long nighttime conversations back and forth, plus their dumping of softball-sized piles of excrement on his lawn. Bill decided to act.

Concerned that this behavior was caused by improper diet, Bill soaked some small sponges in bacon grease, a culinary delight favored by the fair, four-legged street dwellers of Granite City. He dispensed these doggie hors d'oeuvres, and the doggies loved them. Unhappily, their digestive systems did not, and they were unable to pass feces or the sponges onto Mr. Overton's lawn. How sad. They became bloated with flatus and other complications.

Happily, a veterinarian was able to save the dogs from their own stupidity. Somehow, their master figured out what had happened and managed to move away before Bill Overton found a way to feed him, too.

Dogs

My friend Carla is obviously a lover of life and of animals. She has a great idea for people—short of just killing them—who like to harm animals. Carla points out that there are few laws against abuse of animals that don't involve official witnesses, officers and all that. But, you can use what laws there are. Carla says that in most states you can legally seize (gently, please) any dog that sets paw on your property. Call the local animal control folks to come and take the dog to the pound. It takes the owner between twenty and fifty dollars to bail out the dog when you press the trespass charges.

Another tip Carla passes along when you decide to declare an obnoxious dog MIA is to "lose" its rabies-shot tag. This will add some extra bucks to the bailout. Carla says most pounds don't have the time or inclination to identify individual animals, thus forcing the owner to personally drive in to look over the catch of the day.

Be careful when planning this stunt that you take into consideration the owner who might not care enough to buy back the dog, and what happens to the animal if nobody claims it.

I forgot to tell Carla that in their own world, dogs have a pound where they tow stray humans. Sometimes they perform medical experiments on them, in a humane fashion, of course. In any case, beware of any animal hospital whose staff vet is named Mengele.

Dolls

You know those soft-sculptured, adoptable dolls that are the current rage? Take advantage of the fact that some alleged people, including chronological adults, are more attached to these ugly con jobs than to other humans or live, traditional pets.

It gets the old mind to tinkering away in its evil closet.

Here, directly from the mind of Reinhard Wunken, are some suggestions if your mark holds dear a cabbage-head kid:

- Assassinate the thing, using a highly graphic form of attack, e.g., decapitation, dismemberment, crucifixion, etc.
- Have it sexually assaulted by the neighbor's dog, or, if the actual act is impossible to create, a composite photo would be the next best thing.
- Put on a one-scene act from "Joan of Arc" with the kid in the title role.
- Send the kid to summer camp, in Lebanon.

Dopers

The word "dopers" attracts attention. The beauty of this stunt is that it will work well against any jerk or jerkess that you'd like to see in trouble with his parents, boss or other authority figure. It's simple, too. You call the mark's home or work telephone number in hopes the authority figure answers. A bit of research could narrow that to actually happening. Here's a sample of what to say.

"Hello. Is (mark's full name) there?"

Authority figure answers negatively and requests a message. If not, you ask if you can leave a brief message.

"The message is that I paid for my dope and that little creep better deliver it or I'm gonna have some street people [or bikers] rip his/her face off. You got that [bitch, lady, punk or whatever name you wish to use]? I get my dope by tomorrow or that little AIDS bait [relationship] of yours is dead meat."

It is likely this rather one-sided conversation will create some interesting additional conversation when the gist of the call is explained to the mark, proving once again that a milligram of prevention is worth a kilo of cure. In one way or another we have Sid, Chris and UCM to thank for this one.

Driveways

Here's another blast from the brain of the Skull. He saves old, dirty motor oil instead of recycling it through the oil companies as an obedient citizen should. He waits for some dark, rainy night, then spreads five or six gallons of this murky mess on the driveway of his hated mark. It works better if the driveway is slightly sloped, as most are. If Skull ever sells the movie rights to this thing, we could call it *Tarmac the Barbarian.*

Electric Power

Somebody you know running a power trip on you, flexing the ego-bully muscles of a new job, promotion or whatever? Black out this ambition by switching his or her home fuse box or circuit-breaker box into the "power off" mode. Then, padlock or spot-weld the box shut. Blame the Nazis, the KKK, the Democrats or some other cult by leaving a crude note.

Electrical Appliances

Many Haydukery fans suggested this one so it really isn't new. But maybe you'd forgotten it, so pay attention now. You are all aware of the removable power-cord block at the back of many TV sets, small ovens and other appliances. It's called the "interlock."

Select your mark's appliance that you wish to sabotage and unplug the interlock. Using clear nail polish, cover the male pins thoroughly with a good, heavy coating. Let dry. Replace the interlock. The appliance will not operate.

The fun really cuts loose, of course, when the frustrated mark finally takes the inoperable appliance to a service center. Big, big repair bills as well as frustration for the repairperson, as most don't spot the trickery.

Explosives

Another booming expert comes along with a formula to rattle windows. St. Petersburg's Captain Video says to poke a small fuse hole in a Ping Pong ball with an ice pick. Then slice the ball almost completely open, but not totally, at its circumference, using a razor blade. Load the ball with any of the mixtures of explosive we've used in past books. Captain Video says to use a portion of the master mix of one pound of potassium chlorate mixed with three-quarters of a cup of superfine German black aluminum powder. Put some six to nine inches of fuse in the hole and seal the ball with nail polish. Captain Video says this will give you "a cherry bomb unlike any you have ever used."

Feces

According to the Hombre of Justice, human feces mix well with chocolate or coffee ice cream and because of the freezing involved, the odor is eliminated. This stunt gives new meaning to the order, eat shit!

Animal feces has application beyond agricultural manure. Our faithful fan, Babs Barfly, lives near a bunch of pigeons and always scarfs up a fresh supply of their gooey white droppings and stores it, later to be substituted for cracker spread or dip in the mark's kitchen.

"Rabbit pellet cookies are an excellent substitute for chocolate chips ... gets the mark away from all those harmful sweets," she adds.

Financial Fun

The Shadow knows, even if he's from Chicago. Let's say your mark is a heavy gambler and owes money. You get some nasty-voiced goon to call (choose one or more) the mark's best friend, employer, spouse, parents, parole officer, etc., and say something like:

> "Your [friend, spouse or whatever] owes ['Loanshark Eddie' or some other name with real Mob clout in the area] two grand. He says you'll take care of it today personally. So, Crazy Larry and Knucklebuster Spike are gonna be there in two hours to collect the money offa you. Need I say more? Good-bye!"

It takes little imagination to imagine the results of that telephone call.

Food

Consulting the menu from Aunt Nancy's Kitchen, we discover that you can burn your mark if you insert some fun into his or her personal, homemade assembly line of cakes and cookies. The major idea is to ice the baked goods with something yucky. What comes to mind is bacon-grease icing. Try it on your mark's cookies and cakes. Some food coloring should hide the smell.

Would you like to freak out some real rat who has mistreated you to horrible dinners and other meals? Invite him or her to your place, or, better yet, to a neutral location for dinner. Slip a couple of mice or rats into a blender with other ingredients of your choice and make a whipped delight. Put it into a baked shell, pie, quiche or whatever is in at the moment. But be sure to name it.

Let your mark eat it. Whether or not you inform the mark what was eaten, when or how, is up to you.

Sharing food with friends is a popular Yuppie treat. According to Billy Bea McStates, a true Yuppie master, one of the newer trends is to volunteer food from your plate to the plates of others. Here's how Billy Bea does it.

"I slurp up a bite of something, chew it around for awhile, then offer it out, saying, 'Hey, wanna try some of my food?' They think it's gonna be fresh off a plate, least ways until I spit what's been wetly masticated in my mouth onto their spoon or directly onto the mark's plate."

Footwear

Did you ever want to float someone's footwear? Gary Signora found it fun to pee into a beaker, then pour the output into his mark's deck shoe, rubber overshoe or winter boot. Sometimes, he peed into a plastic bag and then fit that inside his mark's footwear.

Why does he do such urinary things?

"A few months ago, my brother left my shoes outside in the rain after he'd borrowed them. I raised hell. He said it would never happen again. Then he gets pissed at me for something and he does it again on purpose. He told me he did it cause he was pissed. What else could I do? I pissed in *his* shoes."

Four Wheelers

Four-wheel drive vehicles are great, useful and valuable. Sometimes, though, idiots obtain these prime vehicles and do rude things to other people's property. This is where CW of Hastings drives in with a great payback.

His is a simple idea that befits the simple-minded Brotherhood of Rednecked Baboons who misuse these fine machines. When the weather is horrible, icy or snowy, or the goon is in a desert dune, simply unlock one of the hubs on his vehicle. He has locked them both and assumes they are locked. You unlock only one. He drives as if his vehicle were in four-wheel drive. It's not. Disaster ahead. Or, behind.

Freaky Stuff

Thank the Shadow for this excursion into the occult. If you want to terrify your mark more than hurt her/him, follow these simple directions. Get to your mark's bedroom window. Take a glass cutter and gently cut a square hole in the glass. Be careful not to cut the whole way through the glass. Choose a biker's glove that is just larger than the hole, or the other way around, and glue it over the cutting on the outside of the window. If you can't get a glove, a photo will do. The idea is that a biker has left his calling card and may reappear anytime.

Scared? I bet your mark sleeps on his or her back for a long time after the stunt ... if sleep comes.

Next freak shot is when you hire a really disgusting and gross person and put him or her in a really disgusting outfit. You are going to take revenge on someone who really irritated you. It could be a former sweetie, boss or whomever.

This person you have hired to do your freaky stunt must be a terrible sight. You must insist that he/she have a *huge* head cold or sinus condition as a prelude to employment. When he/she gets to your mark's home and the mark swings open the door, your disgusting stooge shouts "Boogergram, Boogergram!!!!" and blows his/her nose fully on the mark, pulls the door shut, and leaves as fast as possible.

Furniture

Sherry of Palm Springs has a true vandal's way of getting back at somebody's furniture when the host/hostess or furniture has been nasty to her. For instance, she says if they have a beanbag chair, she makes a small slice in it with her razor-knife. Or, she makes several slices. The weight of the next occupant and gravity will carry this stunt to completion.

Gasoline Stations

Does the pump jockey dribble gasoline all over your car? Does he wipe your windshield with a greasy rag? Was a simple twenty-dollar tune-up upgraded to a fifty-dollar rip-off? Is it any wonder you're not happy with the owner of this service-oriented business?

Simply remove the inspection stickers that your state bureau of measurements puts on the dealer's gasoline pumps to certify that they have been tested and found to be accurate. The station owner will be in REAL trouble if you do that. Do your duty as a good citizen, too, and report to the proper officials that there are no stickers on Mr. Mark's pumps.

Graffiti

Obviously, graffiti are very useful little musings from the walls of toilets, walls, buses, overpasses, etc., and make up the philosophy of America's street scholars. These graffiti also make great slogans for T-shirts, bumper stickers, letterheads or, in their purest form, can be spray-painted on something belonging to your mark.

According to our veteran contributor Geneth, paint pens are the best invention for graffit artists since walls. Geneth says you should always buy the large size, too, as it lasts longer and is cheaper. Paint pens do a neater job and are easier to hide than cans of spray paint.

When the politically controlled Nuclear Regulatory Agency was ordered from the White House to light up Three Mile Island by starting the reactors, some dissident friends of your author scribbled some large painted notices on bridges and other natural billboards along the Pennsylvania Turnpike: "HERSHEY, PA: IT MELTS INTO THE GROUND, NOT IN YOUR HAND."

Here are some prime examples of specific graffiti you can use:

- To all virgins—thanks for nothing!
- When I want your advice, I'll beat it out of you
- When the going gets tough, the tough go drinking (doping)

- When all else fails, lower your standards
- I survived Catholic schools
- It's not pretty being easy
- Life is a bitch, then you die
- Reality is for people who lack imagination
- A woman's place is in the mall
- Cocaine is God's way of telling you that you're making too much money
- When God made man she was only funning
- Yuck Fou
- We'll get along better as soon as you realize I'm god
- Real men don't have floppy discs
- Time flies when you don't know what you're doing
- Life is too important to be taken seriously
- Get stoned, drink wet cement
- I love the immoral minority

Grave Sites

If you really want to spook some primary or secondary mark, mess with the burial site of an appropriate, symbolic, but dead mark. Maybe that one could be referred to as the markee. In any case, Dick Smegma has the answer to this grave question.

He says to pour sulphuric or hydrochloric acid on the grass atop the markee's site. It will kill vegetation more quickly than standard herbicides. I can think of all sorts of fun, secondary things you could add to this stunt to make it really twilight-zone time. I bet you can, too.

Desmond Dosdose is fifty-three years old and has been a hard worker for the past thirty-four years, totally loyal to his company. He was ordered into early retirement at less than a justified amount after his employer sold out for a huge profit within two hours of pledging to employees he would not sell out if they would agree to a wage giveback of 30 percent. The "clever" owner did this to make his business a more attractive sales package. He sold and ran.

Viewing his professional death as being worth a fun, live one, Desmond sought a trusted friend in another state who had another friend who was a stone mason. Some dollars changed hands and a very realistic tombstone was created in the name of the former business owner who'd lied to and cheated his 175 employees. The name and date of birth were correct. The date of death was two months in advance.

The tombstone was photographed and made into postcards. These were sent to the boss who was now "retired" in Florida. A copy was sent to his wife who was still in the Northeast, selling the house and joining him later. In the meantime, the original tombstone was planted in the front lawn of the business.

Would you believe it spooked the new owners enough that final signings were delayed six months, which made it necessary for the former owner to make four very expensive trips back.

In the meantime, several people from all over the U.S., friends of our hero, began to call both the mark and his wife every few days saying, "Only _____ days left to live. Are you ready to die? How does it feel to be a dead man?"

OK, enough light humor, it's back to heavy time. If you really want to shatter your mark, as in "do the sucker in," here you go. Borrow some very uninhibited friends, truck them to the gravesite of your mark's close family. Using a Polaroid camera, have your associates perform sexual and scatological acts upon the grave site and stone, then mail the photos to your mark.

Gross Out

An undeserving couple was nastily undercut by a Yuppie hostess at a neighborhood party. Being only semiwimps, they applied for help from a friend who had graduated from the Haydukery School of Mayhem. Here's what he did.

"I went to the lady's next party as a guest and took a can of instant whipped cream with me inside my coat," recalls Pablo Gorman. "The lady's friends did some very upper-class snotty charades, cutting on poor people, minorities, stuff like that. I got ready for my turn.

"Before going in front of the group, I filled my mouth with the whipped cream. Then, I strode out and stood in front of the hostess. I began to stroke my neck up and down, starting slowly, then going more rapidly. Within a few moments, I moaned, bulged my eyes, opened my mouth and spewed the whipped cream all over her face."

In the climactic confusion, Pablo Gorman quickly left, the message intact.

Gun Dealers

If your potential mark is a federally licensed gun dealer, you can target his posterior in rapid-fire big trouble by reporting him to the Bureau of Alcohol, Tobacco & Firearms, a federal bureau that enforces gun laws, often beyond their letter. Most dealers fear the BATF the way Jewish folks feared the Gestapo in WWII's Germany.

The best way to attract attention to the dealer is to call BATF and tell them the dealer is selling guns without paperwork, selling to kids and fencing stolen guns. Another idea would be to buy an ad in the local newspaper on behalf of your gun dealer/mark and advertise that he sells live machine guns cheap and without all the federal paperwork. Stress in your ad that the dealer has "found a loophole in the fed's stupid law" that lets him sell machine guns freely. Clip the ad and send it to BATF in Washington.

It's true that most gun dealers are very honest, fill-in-all-the-paperwork legal people, so use this stunt only if the mark is a true bastard or crook. The fun can come if your mark is *not* a licensed gun dealer. Better yet, if he or she hates guns, then you have a perfect mark for another BATF scam. Plant weapons and dummy sales records, and make actual sales to hoods in the mark's name, and so on. Then, report Mr. Anti-gun to the feds as an unlicensed dealer.

Guns

After Edgar got ripped off, then physically busted up in a drug deal at his local bikers' bar, he had some fun. Considering that he was going to split for Panama on a permanent basis, he decided to "act" as a purchasing agent for that biker group in making a deal for some "off-paper" street guns, i.e., guns not properly registered and sold. He knew he was dealing with undercover agents of the BATF.

"I set up the deal and pulled in a few of the brothers who had me beat up, letting them think that I was trying to get back into favor," Edgar told me. "I got the deal set, then I split. I learned that four of my former brothers got busted in Maryland on federal gun charges and are going to do about three to five years each. Good news."

Alonzo Hitler bought one of those very realistic-looking replica submachine guns after his boss literally walked away from his gambling debt to Alonzo by pointing a loaded pistol "near" Alonzo's testicles, and telling him the debt was paid.

"Enough of that bull. I got the replica submachine gun and got a girlfriend to drive," Alonzo said. "I knew the boss was out of town for the day so we took his very recognizable Continental from where he'd parked it.

"She was behind the wheel and we drove all over town. I had done a bit of disguise makeup and had dressed the way my boss always dressed so from a distance I looked like him. Every time we came near a crowd, I waved the fake gun out of the car window. People scattered.

"We drove through a mall parking lot and I screamed at a group of senior citizens waiting for their bus, 'Get down or I'll blow your worthless heads off.'"

This went on for only ten minutes as Alonzo and friend figured the police would be beaming along soon. The boss had parked his Continental at the airport which is where Alonzo and his girlfriend left it—thirty minutes before El Jefe's flight was due in.

When the boss landed and walked up to his car, he found several police cars and some very antsy officers waiting for him with their own, very real guns drawn. They wanted to discuss his gun-waving car ride that afternoon.

Airline alibi? The boss had no airline alibi. He had faked the flight and ducked out the side door of the airport to meet his extramarital sweetie in her car for a trip to a nearby motel. She brought him back in time to "come off" the flight and appear to be arriving home to his wife and family. Alonzo knew all of this, of course.

"It took a month and about $1,300 of his lawyer's time to straighten out all of this," Alonzo reports. "I'm not sure how it all came out at home, though. Poorly, I hope."

Hair

You may have to think about this original idea for a few moments to appreciate all the ramifications of disrespect, taboo and mind-mess involved. Put simply, mail hair to your mark. Mail pubic hair or go to a barber shop and collect sweepings of hair. You can be subtle or you can be gross.

One of my milder friends gets back at club or disco bars with bad entertainment and heavy cover charges by pasting pubic hair on the mouths of women pictured on promo posters promoting the band or singers.

If you're a waitress, bartender or customer, you can plant pubic hair in people's drinks and food. Think about the mental anguish. Always pick a good taboo like this for fun revenge on someone's mind. Hair's thinking of you, kid.

Halloween

As a lot of people have known through the years, Halloween is a fine time for having fun with serious intent, i.e., a great time to get even. Suppose your mark lives in one of those security-bound buildings protected by closed circuit TV, guards and all that. Wait until Halloween, when a lot of guests will be entering the building in costume or other disguises.

Have a very trusted friend who has no connection with the mark rent your costume for you. Both of you will need airtight alibis in the event the police get involved, i.e., if your stunt is really awful.

You dress in the surrogate-rented suit and do your dirty work. All that the guards or the video cameras note is "someone" in your costume. Frankly, unless a truly sensational crime is involved, police have more vital things to do than chase down a prankster in a Halloween suit on Halloween night. Although others had the same basic idea, the icon of creation here was Dick Smegma.

When I was a kid, we had this old grump in the neighborhood who was our mark because he was such a mean old prick all year-round. Halloween was our one night to get even and we usually did. But those were the innocent years. Today, new generations would deal with him in a different fashion, as you'll see.

Take advantage of all the media hype about

sickies who poison candy or stick razor blades in kiddies' goodies. This time, *you* or a very trusted friend plant the poison or the blades in your own kid's stash or that of the friend's kid. Make sure you have some witnesses when you "check" your kid's candy as "a concerned parent."

Of course, in your intelligence-gathering stage earlier, you learned what sort of goodies the mark is handing out. Duplicate it. Now, for the surprise—you "find" the doctored stuff and announce that your kid got it from "Mr. Mark." The kid will probably agree, because he or she did get that sort of treat there. Make sure you have removed the other examples of that treat from the bag before "breaking your case."

Call the police. Follow up with a civil lawsuit for millions so you get publicity. Even if all the hype falls through, listen to the word-of-mouth reputation you've created. A good way to poison the old neighborhood well, as it were.

Health
Notice

You need to have professional printing to get this stunt started. That, and human nature, will assure that the stunt works, says Dick Smegma, a master who lost his amateur status years ago. Here's the deal. Get phony forms printed that look as if they're from your state's health department. Use all the official seals, etc. This is why you need to have a friendly printer in your trust.

Use the form to report to your mark that he/she has been sexually active with a partner who has been positively diagnosed as having AIDS. The form should carry the warning, **"Please refrain from sexual relations of any kind until we can diagnose your case."** Tell the mark to bring this form in person to (address of local clinic filled in) on (set a date and time). Include some reference numbers, case numbers, etc. Insist that the mark bring along any spouse or regular sexual partner, too.

The mark will be in a panic, especially if he/she is a straight arrow. It could cause all sorts of fun with spouses, friends, employers, etc. Also, think of the yuks when he/she shows up at the clinic.

High School

A long, long time ago in a galaxy far, far away, when he was a young tad, Colorado's Bill Basque remembers how his and a rival high school cooperated to stop senseless vandalism. Bill says the student councils at the two schools signed a pact saying that the senior class treasury would be used to pay for any damages done to the rival school before, during or after "the big game."

"We had one guy who was a little bit craftier than the rest. He lined up some very sensible damage to our school using the other school's name and colors; then he planted some incriminating personal property evidence he'd managed to acquire from some kids who went to the rival school.

"Naturally, his little counterterrorist stunt caused an uproar, depleted the other senior class's treasury and ruined their senior prom. He was a bright kid. I think he works for the Republican National Committee now," Bill muses.

Homes

Barcelona Blom seems like a nice enough guy. He was kind enough to write me a letter explaining how he moonlights as an interior decorator. Join me as I share some of his professional suggestions.

"I had a guy at work who really screwed me a couple times on borrowed money and was nasty and gloaty about it. I got the biggest Mason jar I could find and filled it with samples of paint, wood stains, glues, old motor oil, ketchup, animal blood, puke and all sorts of nasty crap. Nothing fancy, I just put the lid on, drove it over to the mark's place about 3 a.m. and heaved it through his big picture window right into his fancy living room. About a week later at work he was bitching about his megabuck cleaning bill and that he had no idea who'd be sick enough to do such a thing. I did, but I kept my mouth shut."

Hood Ornaments

While hood ornaments have gone the way of old hoods, I think they are classy and should be resurrected, but with changes. It might be fun to place a dead rat on the front of a mouthy mark's car with a neck tag that reads, "You're next." This particular use of a message for a newly planted ornament came from Shadow.

I, myself, had thought of mounting a stiffly dead groundhog so that my mark's new "hood ornament" stood up, impaled from the animal's sphincter muscle. Perhaps a note would be appropriate, perhaps not.

The only worse use of head ornaments I have heard of came from John "Big Dick The Truck" Camper, who is normally a quiet, poetry-addicted, middle-aged member of a small-town Elk's Club. He told me he would love to find, buy and place a dead human head on the hood of his truck. Does he look in morgues, anatomy classes or Democratic Party rallies?

Hospitals

Dolly Gurney, who toils in the medical profession in West Virginia, has a nasty twist of humor. She offers up some intelligence which might be useful to some of you who have something to repay a hospital for.

Whenever a body (aka a dead person) is being moved from one area of a hospital to another, it is usually loaded onto the bottom tray of one of the double layer carts they use. This makes it look less ominous, I suppose. The body is hidden under a sheet so unsuspecting visitors fresh from seeing Uncle Joe in his last throes of terminal herpes won't be offended by another stiff. To check, look carefully for the white toe-tag clipped to the sheet.

Hospital orderlies haul these loads during their routine rounds. Sometimes, the deceased is unattended for three, four or even five minutes at a time. Sound like part of a comedy film plot? Nope, it's true. How much imagination does it take to list five quick stunts you could pull involving this silent coconspirator?

Dolly revealed an incident from her own medical facility when one of the snooty clerks from the front office, a habitual gossip and confirmed bitch, was standing in the hall flapping her mouth in a torrent of lies about some other employee's sex life. Dolly says one of the orderlies had his buddy assume the corpse position on the lower shelf of the meat wagon, complete with a tag on a bare toe peeking out from under the almost carefully tucked sheet.

Laughing with her usual gusto, Dolly continued, "The orderly was whistling gaily as he approached the bitch and her cornered audience. They looked up and saw what was coming—no big deal. As the orderly drew abreast of the gossip, he slowed almost to a stop as if not being able to pass.

"At that very moment, the other orderly, pretending to be a corpse on the lower shelf, slowly reached his hand out from under the sheet and firmly grabbed the bitch's ankle."

Dolly reports that the shriek was heard from Pittsburgh to Louisville, and that the markess had to change her underwear immediately after she was revived by an ammonia cap.

Yeah, I liked it, too.

Insects

Jennifer Marshall is a grand lady who now lives in California. She's had a bad time because she is good, honest, hard working and good looking. But best of all, she has a grand sense of humor, and she also knows how to use fleas.

She suggests you take three or four plastic storage bags that seal and put a small amount of honey in the bottom of each. Blow some air into each bag. Then, Jennifer says, locate some roaming neighborhood cat that is always outside, i.e., a full-occupancy flea motel. Hold the bag over the cat's back and run the open end along the fur as you pretend to pet it. You will sweep up many fleas into your bag.

Next, take the bags of fleas to your mark's car. If you want the fleas to have a nice home, sprinkle some powdered sugar around the interior of the vehicle, too. This also works for apartments, mail slots, etc.

It may be true that the early worm risks being eaten by a late-night bird, but cockroaches will probably outlive us all. There must be a growing appreciation for cockroaches, though, as both Shadow and The Quarter Machine suggested cockroach eggs as a useful tool for the happy Hayduker. These little eggs, which look just like popcorn kernels, can be gathered from most fleabag apartments and hostels. Some laboratory-supply companies also sell them. They would be a delightful present for that special someone, especially if he or she likes popcorn.

Joggers

While this is actually more a defense measure than a revenge stunt, many people who jog have called when I do talk shows to ask how they can get back at their attackers. Other than the usual bag of after-action goodies, there are always "kicking spikes," sold for general personal defense, but ideal for joggers. Basically, they are 20-gauge steel spikes worn unseen under your shoelaces, but protruding enough to do damage. Kicking spikes are available from Defense Systems, PO Box 297, Awendaw, SC 29429.

Jukeboxes

Nothing fancy, but this stunt could cause the demise of one of these machines, plus the spillover ill will of ear-mushed customers toward the restaurant or bar. Put a bunch of your abandoned change, two or three dollars' worth, into the target box and select the worst song on the play list. Researching the establishment, its patrons and the play list for maximum effect is vital before you attempt this stunt. A bit of test marketing could also help you. Select the absolute worst song, the really aural dog on the list, and pump in all your change. Hit the buttons and leave or stay; either way, enjoy.

Junk
Mail

According to M. K. Smith, the definition of a real loser is a Democrat who gets junk mail with the postage due.

Want your mark to receive lots of junk mail? Write a nice, polite, literate letter in your mark's name to Direct Mail Advertising Association, 6 East 43rd St., New York, NY 10017. Ask them to please place "you" on their master list for merchants and advertisers as "you" dearly love the bargain shopping that comes in the mail to "you." You might also note that you are a shut-in and do your shopping via the mails. Soon your mark will be buried in unwanted advertising. If you want to thank someone for that last idea, wave a hearty hand to little Tommie Titmouse.

The Baffling Radiologist offers a way of fighting back against junk mailers. He makes top-quality Xerox copies of "First Class U.S. Postage PAID" mail labels he gets from junk mailers. He then packs up boxes of ugly and evil things, sticks the labels on them and has them mailed back to the organization of origin by other friends in strange places.

Or, for a bit more money, you can mass-produce counterfeit and/or stick-on labels with your printer pal. Depending upon your legal adviser, this stunt may be illegal. So what? Happy posting.

At long last, the combined forces of that great people's law firm of Hacker and Computer have found a way to smash the evils of junk mail in a very modern way. The firm's eloquent representative, Mr. Master Hacker, Esq., tells it as it should be.

First, find out the name of the "top executive" in the junk-mail company. Then, find out where the main office is and if possible what the telephone prefix (first three numbers) is. Now, you need an efficient, trusted hacker, who knows how to bypass security on the company computer.

Have the hacker delete the entire mailing list, or just a few names if you prefer, yours being one of them, of course. If you feel really devilish, substitute another mark's name for yours or put many different names with his address on the list. Second, order moderate amounts of products in the name of the "top executive" of the junk-mail firm. If the hacker knows what he/she is doing, the executive will never find out what happened.

Another suggestion involves learning the names and addresses of several salesmen or executives, including the main office address of the company. Make a fake chain letter with the list of these individuals and their addresses. In the chain letter, promise that if you send x numbers of dollars to the top person, delete his name, and add your name to the bottom, you will receive x number of dollars when your name reaches the top. Include instructions to make x copies of the letter and send it to x numbers of friends. As you know, chain letters are quite illegal, but you will still follow through with this plan by sending copies of the letter to your friends, who are the postmaster general of the United States, the U.S. attorney general, the local district attorney, and any other law-enforcement personnel you wish to include.

An alternative to the dollar amounts might be to say "send your wife/husband to the man/woman at the top of the list for one night. When you reach the top you will have had x different encounters; some of them will have been great fun."

Ku Klux Klan

Leave it to Dick Smegma to dirty the sheets of this idiotic group of good old boys with a great stunt that uses the KKK as an unwitting aide. Dick says to get a membership application sent to your mail drop in a phony name. Make some color photocopies or have your printer do this for you for later use. Fill out one in the mark's name, use a postal money order for the initial membership fee of about $25, then list the mark's work address or his minister's address or the local "Black Power" organization's address for that of the mark. Mail it back to the Klan.

Landlords

Donna Vicegrip has a friend whose landlord was a real one-man pestilence who finally did an ultimate dirty deed to the tenant families. Donna came to the rescue and here's what happened.

This was a single-family house so the scam was confined to the landlord and was executed as the tenants prepared to leave. The first step is to visit a couple of markets and among other things buy ten or twelve five-pound bags of sugar. Go to a pet store and purchase a bunch of crickets and roaches (they're sold as pet food).

When you return to the house, and in the daytime, carefully turn off all the electricity at the main switch box. Remove all of the wall-light switch plates. Using a common kitchen funnel to guide the flow, pour the contents of each bag of sugar into a different switch hole, directed downward. Place about ten to fifteen of the bugs in each switch hole. Replace the plates and turn the power back on.

The insects will feed on the sugar between the walls and will multiply like bigots in government. The rotten landlord will never get rid of them.

A wonderful fan called in a variation of this stunt during a talk show in Florida. He suggested filling the walls with effluvia, dead animals, vomit, etc., using the electrical access holes as entry points.

If working with bugs makes you crawly, Donna has a modification of the insect invasion.

Again, pull the main block and shut down all of the power in the house. Remove all of the switch plates from the switches and the face plates from the outlets. Cut all wires from all switches and plugs, attach fishhook weights to the cut wires and let them fall to the floor, *inside* the wall. Next, secure the plates in place again, only this time use Superglue to seal the bond so that the screws are just cosmetic. Imagine the landlord's fun when he tries to make the wiring functional again.

Tanya and friends have slumlords under fire in southern California. A feisty lady, she had a friend print some "official" forms, illegally using the name of the landlord, who really is a slime and a slumlord. She makes sure that all new tenants get a copy. The tenant reads the form, reproduced here, and sends it in. Much fun then happens between the landlord and the authorities.

(Date)

Dear Tenant:

It has come to our attention that your apartment building has numerous health and safety violations. As a service, we are providing you with this form so that your rent can be reduced or stabilized if the owner of this building does not upgrade your apartment complex. A list of common complaints follows. Check and comment on those that apply to your apartment.

1. Old, worn carpeting.
2. Broken dishwasher.
3. Broken garbage disposer.
4. Leaks in plumbing, causing mildew, mold, sagging ceilings and/or walls due to water damage.
5. Missing window screens.
6. Unusable underground parking due to poor lighting in the garage area at night.
7. Nonoperating washers and/or dryers, necessitating the use of a laundromat.
8. Peeling paint.
9. Clogged sinks.

Please take the time to fill out the form and list your complaints, then tell us how much less you feel your rent should be because of these defects. We will take legal action if necessary to protect your rights.

Sincerely,
(Name and Title)
Los Angeles Rent Control Board
(Address)

Another way to hassle a landlord is to picket his home, office, other rental properties, or wherever you might locate him/her personally, e.g., his country club. Be sure to include minority pickets and make broad hints that the landlord won't rent to members of ethnic, racial and social minorities. Old people are great sympathy-arousing minorities for this stunt, as are nice young couples with babies whom the landlord has "put out in the cold." Make sure these are all working-class folks and civilized minority types. You will get sympathetic media coverage, too, if you play this properly.

Laundromats

Have one of these absentee-ownership businesses ruined your clothes, ripped you off or otherwise stained your relationship without a hope of mending things in a reasonable fashion? Holy White Tornado, it's Filthy McNasty and Vera to the rescue with myriad grand ideas.

If the laundromat has no attendant on duty, and most don't, simply go into the place and fill all the washing machines with quick-drying cement. This will cost a hell of a lot of bucks to repair. The dryers can be sabotaged by filling them with expanding plastic foam. Best to do this at night when there are no other customers around.

Or, you can walk into the washeteria with about five pounds of calcium carbide (wonderful stuff) and dump it into a washing machine. Start the cycle and run like hell. It will foam up like crazy, give off an incredibly obnoxious-smelling gas, and also gum up the machine's gears.

These are drastic measures. Here is a lightweight goody. Most laundry detergents are a white powder. So is powdered bleach. Buy a box of Tide, or similar laundry soap, empty out half of it, and fill it with powdered bleach. Leave the box behind. If this is used for colored clothes, they will run beyond belief. Some laundry detergents are a green or blue powder. So is dye. Mix in some dye with the colored soap powder. Guess what happens?

Another way to point out the errors of their

ways to errant owners of these establishments comes from an old Vietnamese friend of mine, a laundryman named Diddy Mao. He converts empty washing machines and clothes dryers into pet cages. For instance, he suggests you put a large, live rat into one of the washers and close the cover. Or, fill one of the machines with crickets from a bait shop, or a swarm of bees. In any case, the customer is going to be the secondary mark in this sting and will surely be out to spread some legal venom to the owner of the business.

Lights

Here's a quickie from Jolly Cholly Potter, who likes to put shoe polish on the pull-strings hanging down from basement light fixtures. Calling into one of my talk shows, he said, "I do it to my girlfriend a lot and she always falls for it. It's a real hoot, as the old mark gets polish all over his or her hand."

He's in the coal business if that helps explain things.

Local Officials

Political philosopher Fearing Pangborn, director general of the Albanian Human Rights Council, mistrusts both the U.S. and the USSR war-monger governments. Speaking of them in tandem, he notes, "Facts without theory is trivia, while theory without facts is bull." All of which brings up this great scam played on small-town bozos.

The hero is very careful not to give away anything of his identity to us because he's still having too much fun to even risk getting caught. But it's all true. Basically, what he let me know so far is that a small community's "old boy club" leaders screwed him badly on a business deal in favor of one of the old boy's sons, using insider data via the local bank president. Nasty business. Much of the blame goes to the police chief and the mayor who brought blackmail pressure on the banker because of his extramarital affair with a local lady. The lawyer who gained big bucks was the mayor's son.

Our hero had a friend in another town across the country get him a fine transceiver with the local police and emergency frequencies on it, including the scrambled tactical operating frequencies. He had another out-of-state friend wire a connector between his transceiver and his car's cassette player.

Our hero rides around the area at odd hours of the day and night playing quick snatches of porno cassettes featuring very explicit sound effects. He precedes the tape selection with a recorded cut-in done by another out-of-state friend who can imitate Johnny Carson and the voices of other stars, saying things like, "And now, dear friends, here is my on-the-spot recording of the mayor's daughter whoring around with the police chief's mother."

Naturally, in a small town, all sorts of gossip about this has started, and our hero has become a folk hero to an underground newsletter started by an out-of-work bunch of labor-union folks who also have justified grudges against the power elite of the town.

Not only can you use a transceiver with the proper crystals or frequencies to have fun in official radioland, you can also modify the official actions of the minions of this land. As Jake Buckshot explains, "I got an official transceiver through a buddy who had been a cop until he tired of the 'bash first, ask later' mentality in his town and moved on. I use it to cut in on stupid dispatch orders.

"We had some bluenoses upset about a nude section of public beach up here. They pressured the local police into hassling these quiet folks who felt like sunning and swimming without suits. I decided to help out these dumb Nazis we got here playing cop."

"I cut into and overrode the dispatcher—I'm a ham operator and radio buff and know how to soup my set—and said, 'Disregard previous instructions, beach squad. Return to base for visual instructions.'

"Another time I sent them to the mayor's house for a reported orgy on the lawn, only I didn't tell them the mayor lived at that address."

Lunch-Bag Thieves

If you're having problems with other folks stealing your brown-bagged lunch at school or work you might want to think about the rather extreme methods José Cajonés took to combat them in his factory job area.

He bought some little discs of moth killer that come wrapped in plastic packs and look somewhat like candy. He wrapped a few in the desert section of the lunch his wife packed and put the lunch on his shelf above his desk. Bingo!

When the fellow employee was taken ill suddenly and had to leave the shop for a trip to the emergency room, José figured his problem was solved. And, it was. Watch your dose rate with this one, though, as a wimp/mark could get really sick.

M.A.D.D.

Because they are such a vindictive bunch of hens, the Mothers Against Drunk Driving must be treated with caution, much as one would approach a poisonous snake. Our contributor on this one will remain fearfully unknown, except for being from the state of Washington. Here's what happened.

A local M.A.D.D. member believed our contributor was a drunk driver because this person worked in a tavern. Our contributor was constantly bombarded with phone calls, mail and visits by M.A.D.D. zealots. Later, a mistaken identity in a local paper caused her more grief with these menacing mothers.

Late one night, our contributor called the local M.A.D.D. busybody's home, gave a fake name and said she was drunk and needed a ride home.

"I gave her the name of the bar and a generic description of myself. I waited for her nearby. While she entered the bar looking for me, I quickly spirited a half empty bottle of booze into her car, with the lid loose," our contributor reports.

"After waiting a few minutes she left, probably figuring it was a prank. In the meantime, I had called the local DWI hotline and reported her car and license. The cops stopped her and found the bottle. We have an open-bottle law in our state, so she was had.

"You know the wonderful there-is-justice-afterall in this matter? She really was legally loaded ... a .17 reading. Ain't it wonderful?

Getting even is such fun," our contributor writes.

Meanwhile, a friend of mine, El Coronel Tomas Eructo, is starting an organization known as Drunks Against Mad Mothers, or D.A.M.N. Would I lie?

Mail

Did you ever want to run a direct-mail business? Did you ever want to run a truly gross direct-mail business? Did you ever consider setting up your mark in just such a business? If you answered "yes" to any of the three questions, read on. Otherwise, turn on your TV and watch the PTL Club's Dollar Flagellation Hour.

All you need to do to put your mark in business is buy a couple of ads in the classified sections of some of the sleazy magazines on sale at your local newsstand or sold through the mail. Set up your mark in the business of providing sex by mail or by telephone. Offer a free first call or something else to shill the customers. Be sure to make your ad copy as lustful as possible, especially if your mark is female. Most guys really run their logic circuits on overload if they think they're going to score for free with a whore-at-heart. Take advantage of this natural biological weakness which occurs in the male species.

Do you need to get someone on a lot of mailing lists or to flood them with samples, introductory offers and subscriptions? There is at least one company that provides all the ammunition for this valuable weapon in your trickster's arsenal. It's called Executive Management, and you will be using their "Direct Media Card Deck" division.

Using a selected nom de mark, order one of the "decks." What you'll get is a plastic-packed deck of direct-mail inquiry cards from various businesses offering myriad services and products. All are pre-addressed to your mark and most have prepaid postage. All you do is select appropriate cards, check a few boxes, then mail. They have a lot of different "deck" selections, as this is a clearing house for promotions, so work this gold mine well and often.

At last, I've finally discovered a positive use for advertising circulars, i.e., you can help your enemies by ordering self-help books for them. Here's the idea. Rob your mark's mailbox of fliers from book-clearing remainder houses, sales outlets, and liquidation sales centers. You then use the adhesive stickers on the order blank to "order" books for your mark on a COD basis.

You can add insult to injury by selecting books that slap the mark's ego, e.g., *30 Days to a Real Bustline, Flatten that Fanny, Home Cure Your Herpes.* You get the idea. Or try to pick books that are totally inappropriate to your mark's lifestyle, biases, etc.

On another scale, the postal one, here is a stunt that is hardly new and dozens of people have suggested it so I imagine it is working well. Let's share it with the rest of the masses. Here's how to mail letters to friends for free. Simply reverse the sender and the sendee name/address locations as per the sketch below, and use no postage stamp.

```
+--------------------------------------------------+
| Actual recipient                                 |
|                                       No stamp   |
|                                                  |
|                                                  |
|                                                  |
|          Your name and address or a fake one     |
|                                                  |
|                                                  |
|                                                  |
+--------------------------------------------------+
```

And speaking of envelopes, you can always use a good supply of postage-paid envelopes, according to governmental consultant Joseph Porta. Joe suggests you shop for a supply of these at government and military offices, corporate mailrooms, etc. He says using these with some commonsense security guidelines really cuts down on your postal bills.

Here's a nice twist on the old change of address bit. This idea came from my old mail delivery man. Either change the mark's address or give the mark a new address, using the existing address of some outfit like the Red Cross, YMCA or whatever. Or, you can change the address of the YMCA, Red Cross, etc., to your mark's home or business address. Whichever you do, the idea is to bury the mark with high-volume mail delivery. The confusion of getting all of this straightened out will be a delight, too.

Microwaves

At first, Dick Smegma's landlord was a nice guy. Then it became obvious that the heel was trying illegally, immorally and however else to force Dick and his wife out so he could rent to a relative. Things got kind of tight and nasty.

"You could feel the tension cooking," Dick noted with glee as he recalled the revenge he extracted.

"We loaded up the apartment's microwave with all the silverware in the place and turned it on for an hour. This act causes the microwaves to feed back into the uranium diode (the heart of the unit), shorting it out and rendering the whole microwave useless."

A quick check with a local repair person netted me the knowledge that repair or replacement of this diode and retuning the unit would cost between $200 and $500.

Molestation

If your mark really deserves this, do it, because the current atmosphere is right and the dirt is ripe for results. Call your mark's employer, or have a lady friend who is a good actress do it. It works well if the mark is a teacher or has some other occupation that involves kids. Tell the employer that the mark made sexual advances to your kid—cry or shake the voice a bit—and you want it stopped. You don't want the police involved because you don't want the child subjected to that, you just want it stopped. See why the caller has to be a good actor or actress?

As a slight variation, Mr. Justice, our clever contributor, suggests you call the employer and pretend to be a vice cop. Inform the employer about a complaint against the mark and that you're checking to see if there have been other complaints. Insist you are trying to keep this quiet and contained.

Motion Pictures

Giggi Taveras was accused of sneaking booze
into a theater when it was actually the people
behind him. He had had a few beers before the
flick so he did smell of booze, but he had *not*
brought in any. He didn't even know the people
behind him. Nonetheless, the manager had him
charged. The fine was twenty-five dollars and
nine dollars in costs. Giggi was furious.

When he next went to the movie, he prowled
around the projection booth and found a lot of
ventilator holes. He noted that with a piece of
telescoping antenna and some putty he could
adjust the sound volume control on the movie
without the operator seeing him as that employee
was also the ticket taker who had other duties after
he set the film to running.

Giggi waited until they showed a good
suspense film. Ten minutes into the film he
stepped unnoticed to the air hole and adjusted the
volume all the way up with his antenna. He
quickly shortened it and was in his seat in three
seconds. After six repetitions of the volume
mysteriously going up and down drastically
within twenty minutes, the show was stopped, the
patrons waited ten minutes for an equipment
check, then the film began again. So did Giggi, the
moment the projectionist left the booth. The next
time, he bravely adjusted the sound while the man
was in the booth but had his back turned. He did
it again. And, again.

By this time the audience was unruly to the point of being surly. The manager stopped the show and not only refunded everyone's money but issued a free pass to all customers for a future movie. Giggi left a pleased and vindicated man. He made sure that he thanked the manager personally with a big smile.

Musical
Cards

Are Father's Day, Grandma's Day, Ex-Spouse Day, and all of the other sentimental holidays really historic or are they just an accumulation of marketing scams by greeting-card companies? Bring up the music maestro, let's explore the issue. Ah, the hell with it. Here's what you do. You know those expensive cards with little mechanical music-makers inside that play some sappy song when you set them off? Set off a whole bunch of them in a store . . . as in a concert of cacophony.

Musicians

Mel tells this great story about her fiancé, Gary. He played in a group with a piano pounder who was a thorough rotter. Nobody liked the guy and he earned this hatred every day because of his ego and actions. Gary decided to have some professional fun.

"They were in a stage setup where Gary was playing guitar behind and below where the keyboard was set up. Gary waited until the piano jerk had a solo, then crawled to the bench, totally out of sight of the audience, and slipped his body just under the man's bench. Then, with his drumstick he started to beat a completely different tempo back and forth, like a metronome, on the player's knees. Within moments, the man's distractedness showed and he hopelessly fouled up his solo. The audience got very restless. Nobody in the group jumped in with a riff to save him, either. He took another long, long minute to finish his messed-up solo," Mel reports.

Newspapers

Not long ago, the Wilkes-Barre, Pennsylvania, *Times Leader,* which presumably employs editors and proofreaders, reported the wedding of Thomas Durkin and Mame Broody. According to the paper, the wedding party included people with names like Gloria Snockers, Lilac Arug, Amos Behavin, and Hugh G. Wrection.

At about the same time, the Columbia, South Carolina, *Record* published an employment agency's classified ad in the help-wanted section under "Secretary." It read: "Several Positions w/ Top Co. Screw Your Way to the Top!"

Both items were obviously the work of jokesters, the kind of thing newspapers hate, but Haydukers love.

No Parking Zones

Our old pal Trusty Giusti on the West Coast doesn't like lazy jerks who park in handicapped zones. He has large, newsprint signs printed and fixed with stick-on glue backing. His sign is a foot square and he slaps them right in the driver's vision zone of the windshield of the offending parked vehicle. The sign says "Don't park in handicapped zone again, jerk, or we'll see that you qualify!" He reports that the signs are very difficult to remove.

One Liners

These are good, tested one-liners that you can use to put down or otherwise top another person during a public confrontation that has attracted the attention of other folks. The decibel level at which you deliver the line will reflect on the situation. Also remember that timing is vital to effective communication.

- It doesn't matter if you're gay (to a person of the opposite sex).
- My God, *he* got you pregnant?
- Stay the hell away from my ten-year-old daughter! (to an older man)
- You shouldn't even be in here—you have herpes (in a restaurant, bar or child-care center).
- Keep your hands off my ass (anyone of either sex).
- Don't you dare follow me to the bathroom again, you fag!
- My God, you're carrying a gun!
- Goddamn it, you're a narc. Hey, he/she's a narc (great in a biker bar).
- Deny you're a narc, you jerk (also great in a biker bar).
- How can you sell dope that cheap? (anywhere, but great in schools)

I am sure you have others that you've used in the past. I'd like to hear about them. For these, I wish to thank Warthog, M. N. Chunder, Dick Smegma and Carla.

Paint

As a journeyman painter, Skull introduces us to a fine product known as "Fix Quick" or "Fix All," depending upon the brand name. It is used to fix deep cracks in drywall or wood. Skull says it can be used to fix creeps as well.

These products come in powdered form to be mixed with water. What might happen if the water you mixed the powder in was in your mark's toilet bowl at the time? Or, pour some of this magic powder into a garbage disposal, sink, drain or washer. Add a bit of water and within fifteen minutes the stuff expands and becomes hard as Sheetrock.

By the way, those little plastic bubble paints that some hobby stores carry team up very well with a heavy-duty, field-model slingshot to do some colorful damage to all sorts of property. This helpful household hint comes from interior decorating hobbyist Mac Barfo.

Parking

Here is an interesting modification to the old "Reserved—Police Dept." bags that people used to carry in their cars to insure parking spots or to beat meters. I heard this stunt down at a local Sons of Mussolini meeting a few months ago. You go to your printer and have a hundred or so cardstock signs made saying "Funeral Parking Only." You can tie these around parking meters all around your mark's store, and customers will stay away. The mark will be afraid to remove the signs because they say in small type at the bottom: "By Order of (town name) Police Department. Do Not Remove."

A friend of mine had a lot of fun with the police department in another town by having his friendly printer make him several books of parking violation tickets that duplicated the originals from the town in question. My friend spent a lot of funny days and evenings issuing them to secondary mark's vehicles. In addition to indiscriminate ticketing, he always dropped a few on some of the police's more outspoken critics in the community to stir the pot of paranoia.

Parking Meters

Will someone tell me if this is possible? Chris Schaefer asks if realistic decals could be made that would match your community's parking-meter windows. You stick them over the expired sign and it would look on routine inspection as if there were money in the meter. Sounds like a grand idea. I asked one printer and he said it surely could be done, but would cost more than the parking was worth unless you were buying in bulk and selling them to the public. Any comments?

Parties

Speaking of party poopers, we have to thank Long Beach's Tanya, a chemist, who suggests that you can use an eye dropper or other small insertion device to put croton oil, a diarrhea producer, or Lasix, a potent diuretic, in chocolates or any other food. It takes a deft touch, Tanya says, but you can do it. She suggests you use your imagination to produce other surprise fillers, then combine with previous Haydukery, like nailing or gluing shut the bathroom facilities.

Refinement is an amusing word to use here considering what's about to happen, but this is a refinement on a stunt from one of the earlier books. A former state legislator offers the idea of a nationally advertised party for bikers to be held at your mark's home. Try to choose some date you know the mark will be there—the wedding of a son or daughter or a neighborhood party—or perhaps you can assure the mark will be there through some pseudo planning of your own.

Then you advertise the party in some biker magazine promoting free beer, food and lots of horny ladies. I suggest *Easy Riders* as I know the magazine well and it has credibility. Include in the classified ad that this is a "coming home party for some righteous brother who's just gotten out of the joint." Give a definite time, date and address.

Even if the "former state legislator" doesn't know for sure, I will guarantee from my background that this one could cause the sudden call-up of the National Guard. I would love to be there. Let *me* know when and where.

Patriotism

Here comes a roaring broadside from Dick Smegma that makes use of patriotic flag-waving. This one works even better if your mark is a super-patriotic son of the Jessie Helms ilk.

Tie an American flag to one end of a rope and tie the other end of the rope to the underside, not the bumper, of the mark's car. Stuff the flag under the car where it cannot be seen. When the mark drives off, Old Glory unfurls and you can guess the rest. Hint: Using the stunt in a high-visibility area adds both risk and more likelihood of the mark getting nailed legally and otherwise.

Pet Owners

The immortal battle: what to do to the rude owners of those dogs who take those gross dumps on your lawn. Rob from Palm Beach got a large box, filled it with packing, then included a plastic bag full of two or three days accumulated dog dump. He sent it to his neighbor COD via UPS from a nearby town. Within four days, the neighbor began to carry a pooper-scooper when he walked his dog.

Philadelphia Parking Tickets

Our madman, Stud McCutcheon, is correct when he says that only folks in the Great Rust Belt of the Northeast will have heard of the infamous Philadelphia Parking Ticket Scam, which he blames on the evil La Croix Brothers Mob. However, the principle is useful anywhere. It seems the Philadelphia traffic-ticket system spews out tickets for people who've never even been in Philadelphia, let alone operated an automobile there. Dead folks have been cited.

Here's how Stud's scam works. You call your mark and identify yourself, let's say as Sgt. McGregor of the (fill in a city or town—perhaps even Philadelphia) Traffic Court Division, and you ask the mark what he or she is going to do about $150 in outstanding traffic warrants.

I am sure you can imagine the rest of the conversation if the mark has never been to the community in question. Nonetheless, adopt a tough-cop attitude and bully the mark. Insult the mark. Threaten the mark. Either frighten the mark or make him/her furious. This one has a lot of sharp edges to it. You can lend authenticity to this by having an associate with the proper accent and attitude make the call.

Pie in the Face

Continuing with his genius of adding new style to old tricks, Dick Smegma brings his scatological outlook on marks into play again. Instead of using a shaving-cream filler to pie your victim, Dick says to make an excrement pie. He also says to mush it in the mark's face; don't just throw it. This works best with wimps or with people who are slower runners than you are.

Pilots

Our Jimmy Carter is not the same honest wimp who was driven from the White House by the histrionics of that Teflon-coated California pond scum. Our Jimmy is a fun guy. When he was hassled by an airplane pilot for reasons beyond belief, Jimmy didn't ground the guy with a fist to the face, he used a blow to the brain.

"I found a book that documented airplane crashes with a lot of really grisly pictures. I made photocopies of the wreckage, the people and the carnage in general and sent them to him as photo postcards," Jimmy reports.

The book Jimmy refers to is *Plane Crashes,* by Beryl Frank (NY: Bell Publishing Co., 1980).

Politicians

We were seated one evening discussing ferals when it wasn't long until Sr. Estercolero Pope mentioned politicians. He said that medical researchers are considering using them for experiments instead of laboratory rats because politicians are more plentiful, they have a metabolism close to that of humans, plus the technicians don't become as emotionally attached to them.

Years ago, Drew Pearson observed that "rarely will a politician pass any law to which he is subject. . . . Most are moral cowards." But that's no reason we cannot imitate them. You've seen Ron Smith's commercial lookalike celebrities on television. These are everyday folks who look and, sometimes, sound like celebrities, but who rent themselves out for a whole lot less than the real issue. The biggest broker in the country for this service is Ron Smith, with offices in New York and Los Angeles (see "Sources").

Why not rent someone who looks and sounds like your least favorite political thing and have your impersonator make political speeches, public appearances, press conferences, etc. The legal key is never to actually identify the actor as the real person. Let the media and audience assumption do the job for you. Never deny, just never formally identify. You can have a lot of fun with this.

If you need someone to thank for this kindness, say "Hi" to Marla and Melanie, twin dynamos of creativity in Phoenix. As Marla points out with a sly smile, "Everytime I see Ronald Reagan on television, I am reminded of that famous line from the *Wizard of Oz*, 'Pay no attention to the man behind the curtain.'"

Porno

Since Adam and Eve went out of the adult photofinishing service, you folks need a safe place to send your sexually explicit photos for processing, the first step for some Haydukery. Here is a good outfit: Male Order Photolabs, 18718 Ventura Blvd., Tarzana, CA 91356. They accept credit cards, too.

Posters

It's not very original, but when a truly stupid local politician irritated Paul W. Ass, and rational discourse didn't settle things, our hero waited two years until reelection time. By this time he had collected some amusing candid photos of the incumbent idiot in silly, semi-embarrassing postures. He used them to illustrate posters that falsely advertised the politico/mark's radical views on unpopular issues. The operable word here is "false" views.

"I put these posters, which cost less than twenty-five cents each from a sympathetic printer, in really high-traffic areas where it is illegal to post posters, like turnpike booths, city trash cans, church windows and service display boards," Paul reports.

When it comes to anti-poster planning, consider the problems faced by an unpopular cause in America—peace. James Idare, a longtime advocate of peace, laments, "Every time we put up posters, some Yuppies, hawks or retreads for Reagan tear them down. I finally had a fine idea.

"I mixed some rather rough ground glass, a bit of cow urine and another chemical in with the paste we used to secure the posters. I figure that trading some poster-ripping for those jerks' fingertips and some later disease is fair enough."

Pricks

According to a story I read in the *Christian Crusade Enquirer,* a California husband who had found a new sweetie instructed his wife to sell all their community property and said they'd split the total. He even agreed to let her sell the true love of his life—his vintage Porsche. He'd rather have it end up with a stranger than with his soon-to-be ex.

Later, she gave him a check for his share, and an itemized receipt. She'd gotten a good price for everything—except the Porsche, which she'd sold to a migrant worker for $75.

This demonstrates to me that the wages of sin vary a whole lot. Or, in the words of the late Bruno McManmon, *saepe intereunt aliis meditantes necem.* For those not conversant in Latin, that means those who plot the destruction of others, often destroy themselves.

Public Smokers

A lot of public elevators have ashtrays to encourage those vermin who smoke among us. Replace the sand in these ash trays with a mixture of potassium nitrate and sugar. Thanks, Barney Vincelette. While we agree very strongly, I'm glad you talked me out of using claymores.

Quiz

There is a short, self-help quiz to tell you if you are a sucker, a victim or someone likely to be screwed by the various bad bullies of our world. Answer "yes" or "no" to these questions.

1. Do work and salary make you free?

2. Do you think Pepsi, your own PC/videogames, vacation outside the fifty states and a five-digit price-tag car represent the good life?

3. Do you give a hoot about the First Amendment?

4. Do you know what it is?

5. Do you really think Jesus moved that rock all by himself?

6. Can the local police really protect your rights?

7. Is capitalism compatible with communism?

8. Is either compatible with humanism?

9. Should R. Reagan and S. Stallone lead the first wave ashore in Nicaragua?

Quotes

Here's some honesty. The first time Mac Chunder and I discussed using quotes in a book, it was as filler. Frankly, we used them to fill up space, to pad the book. To our amazement they have drawn a lot of positive mail, including you folks sending in favorite quotes and quoters.

Make good use of these quotes in your graffiti cryptic messages, threats, bon mots, comebacks, etc.

"The next best thing to a good friend is an enemy who knows you all too well."

—Chester the Spoon

"The easiest way to change history is to become a historian."

—Rev. Jerry Falwell

"The world is absolutely out of control now and is not going to be saved by reason or unreason."

—Robert Lowell

"Somewhere, something incredible happened in history—the wrong guys won."

—Norman Mailer

"Treason never doth prosper; what's the reason? Why if it prosper, none dare call it treason."

—John Harrington

"Conscience is a larger foe of mankind than is gunpowder."

—Snakeoil Cignetti

"We damn Americans roam the world strewing death, destruction and riches in our wake and turn whole countries into either napalmed ruins or flourishing whorehouses."

> —A Vietnam combat vet in protest
> of the U.S. outrages in Nicaragua

"He's such a pacifist you just want to kill him."

> —M. Kerri Smith

"The best political weapon is the weapon of terror. Cruelty commands respect. Men may hate us. But, we don't ask for their love; only for their fear."

> —Heinrich Himmler

"The people will always attempt to find the positive aspects of all circumstances, which, in themselves, are not susceptible to danger."

> —Joseph Stalin

"People aren't really poor until they start using water on their corn flakes "

> —Nancy Reagan

"Great spirits have always encountered violent opposition from mediocre minds."

> —Albert Einstein

"It's better to remain silent and be thought a fool than to speak and remove all doubt."

> —George Bush

"No one can make you feel inferior without your consent."

> —Eleanor Roosevelt

"A dog is a dog, except when he is facing you in a narrow alley. Then, he is Mr. Dog."

> —Nicaraguan street vendor

"Whoever said money can't buy happiness isn't shopping in the right places."

> —Nancy Reagan

"Capitalism gives all of us a great opportunity if we seize it with both hands and hang on to it."

—Al Capone

"Everyone needs to believe in something. I believe I'll have another beer."

—LTC Mac

"It will be a great day when our schools get all the money they need and the Air Force has to hold a bake sale to buy a bomber."

—An American doctor viewing
a bombed-out village in El Salvador

"Too much of a good thing can be wonderful."

—Mae West

"Je te pisse au cul."

—A French veteran of Bergen-
Belsen to Ronald Reagan

"To profess principles but not be prepared to back them is to be without principles."

—Mary J. Berg

"My mother-in-law told us she always had a desire to be buried at sea. I told my wife we should dump her off the Salmon River bridge tonight . . . she'd eventually get to the sea. Three weeks later I'm divorced."

—G. Barrett, via George McGeary

"A fellow who is always declaring he is no fool usually has his suspicions."

—Wilson Mizner

"Ask a kid what he wants for dinner only if he's buying."

—Fran Lebowitz

Radar

You remember how in WWII Allied aircraft dumped tons of aluminum strips to confuse German radar so that millions of these fake blips hid the real blips of the bombers on Nazi radar screens. Fast forward today, courtesy of Gary Sisco.

If you don't like American policy in Latin America, where they bomb villages every day, or you want to screw up a SAC airfield, your own local field or mess up the local police, pay heed to Gary.

"Invest about sixty dollars in a tank full of helium and about five hundred balloons. Fill each balloon and have friends tie strips of aluminum foil to each one. Release them in the area of the airfield where you want to mess up the radar. It works with presto wonderful efficiency all of the time."

He mentioned using vans and other mobile launching units to really mess up things.

Radical Groups

Have a bone to bash with the KKK, MOVE or some other group of dangerous mental midgets? Here's an idea based on something a chap named Chucky Gorman did when he got home from Vietnam.

"I found out the home phone numbers of about a dozen members of the local radical group of hate-mongers. I also knew their leader and how he spewed hatred of anyone who had a job, was white or had white friends, etc. It was a black version of the KKK. I could also imitate his voice.

"All of these brothers got this heavy-duty alert phone call from me about ten o'clock that night, telling them to unearth their pieces. I also told them to bring the heavy stuff—the full autos and sawed-off shotguns—for a big blast-off for some Klanners. I told them to meet me at a specified location at midnight.

"My next call went to the state police and I used my 'Mr. Charley P. Whitey' voice for that call. I told them when and where. Man, I checked out a couple of the brothers and at 11:30 they were loading up their cars and going out for full combat."

Radio-Controlled Aircraft

Every kid wishes he had one ... even us old farts who had to make do with balsa wood gliders dozens of years ago. But now, Mac Chunder's old pal Jimmy Carter has some new uses for the latest in radio-controlled aircraft models.

It's expensive to sacrifice these aircraft, but Jimmy feels if the fault and the cause are enough, then the cure is $$-justified. That works for me. Here are some of his suggestions:

- Always be sure you have included the primary or secondary mark's full name, address and telephone number on an ID plate on the aircraft.
- Crash or land the aircraft in or on the area of a ball game, concert, religious gathering, graduation, funeral, etc.
- Add a smoke or mild pyrotechnic capability to the crash.
- Fly it through the mark's window kamikaze style. This ending works well with corporate windows, trustee meetings, parole boards and union or management gatherings. Again, remember smoke or pyrotechnics.

Radio Stations

C. F. Riggs tells how a friend got back at a local radio station that had fired him unjustly. The gimmick is to buy a stadium or gym seat just as close to the radio broadcasting booth as possible. Take a ghetto blaster to the event. To protect yourself from physical harm by other fans close by, disconnect the speaker. Now, you're ready to do it.

Turn the machine up as high as it will go. Turn the tone control to maximum treble. Carefully tune your radio to the station doing the play by play. The wonderful squeal of feedback will roll across the airways and into the immediate crowd area. Classy!

Recipes

The famed Eastern European chef Job Trojemadj once had a supposed friend pilfer and use two of his personal recipes to win an important culinary skills contest with both monetary and professional rewards at stake. Needless to add, our wronged captain of the kitchen dealt his own set of cards.

"I had printed some blank recipe cards just as my former friend used in his own files. I then prepared some carefully faked recipes with various bogus things, ranging from ingredients to amounts of ingredients, scattered throughout. I had these smuggled into his personal recipe file at his home—items he would prepare for personal guests. It took only a month for the rumors to surface about this man losing touch with his craft," Job Trojemadj reported with obvious savor to his voice.

"Revenge in my field is always a case of hoping for the best, but always expecting the worst," he adds.

You could easily take this stunt another step and use this basic idea to infiltrate bogus recipes into the appropriate locations at stores, restaurants, flea markets, local newspaper columns, etc.

Restaurants

Who else but Dick Smegma would have the fortitude to pull this off, other than me, of course? Dick writes from Hawaii that an "all you can eat salad bar" restaurant had really screwed him over on a business deal. All efforts at civilized collection failed. Haydukery followed.

Dick went to Mission Row, that's Hawaii's answer to Skid Row, and rounded up eighteen derelicts that used to look like humans. He announced he was treating each to a free meal, and he was sincere. He trucked them to the offending restaurant and ordered eighteen "all you can eat salad bar" meals for his odoriferous charges, then paid the $2.50 per each in advance.

"The manager came storming out when he heard the noise and smelled the stench of my guests. He told us to leave, not even offering a refund at first," Dick related. "I pointed out the possibility of both legal action and a very likely trashing of his place by pissed-off bums. He saw the light and had us seated."

Dick reports that the eighteen derelicts stayed for the next two hours, gorging on everything not tied down. Word somehow got out to the washed public that day and they stayed away like fans at a Pittsburgh Pirate baseball game.

When the last of his new friends farted loudly enough to flush commodes a block away and then knocked a painting sideways with a mighty belch, Dick and his guys left. But not before he promised the manager that since they'd had so much fun and fine food, they'd be back again the next weekend.

"The manager and I had an instant settlement of (1) all the money due me for the initial rip-off, (2) refund of my meal money for the eighteen bums, (3) an overall apology, and (4) free luncheon for me for a month on the premise that I not bring back my eighteen friends," Dick reports.

What Dick didn't tell the manager is that he could always find eighteen *new* friends if the need arose again.

Another way Dick got back at a restaurant that had screwed him was to share his story with others in the dining public. He had a printer run off one thousand handbills written and printed in newsletter format explaining how he had been offended by this restaurant and the legitimate ways he had tried to make right his case. He stood outside the restaurant on a public sidewalk and handed the papers to each person heading into the eatery. Dick says the restaurant owner fired the offending manager (who had been a real prick to the help and to other customers) and made amends with Dick personally.

Salad Bars

You really can have a lot of fun getting back at eateries that mess you up or over. Dick Smegma suggests a fun game to play when they have a salad bar.

"Go in, pay, fill up your plate with a lot of messy stuff and begin to eat. Eat with noise, looking, sounding and acting like a pig. It works better if you are personally none too clean," Dick suggests.

"Halfway through, when there is a crowd at the salad bar, come up and say, just after belching loudly, 'I guess I wasn't as hungry as I thought and besides this stuff tastes like Arab snot!' Then, start shoving the leftover food *off* your plate and back into the salad-bar containers."

I would suggest you not look at the horror on the faces of your fellow dining companions as they back away. You'll probably laugh.

Salespeople

Even if they are rude, boorish, pushy and invade your privacy, don't dispose of door-to-door salespeople with a slam in the face of your door. They can be helpful in your never-ending quest for justice against some nasty mark who has wronged you. Here is how James Rodger sees it.

"I politely explain that I cannot afford the product or am just not in the market now. *But,* I do have a friend who has mentioned so many times how much he/she wants a (whatever the salesperson is peddling). Give out the mark's name, address and telephone number. Then you mention something personal.

"My friend was in a severe accident some years ago and has a steel plate in his/her head. Sometimes, he/she gets odd flashes of strange behavior and can be confused. Most of the time, though, my friend is a warm, loving person," is the Rodger pitch. "You might want to call several times to catch my friend in one of the good moods. I just know you'll have a good sale there, as he/she is as rich as can be."

What salesperson could pass up that challenge?

Signs

You can either get one custom-printed or you can borrow a "DANGER—You can be killed!" warning sign from a construction site. The idea, according to Wolfgang Creutzfeldt, is to plant the sign, which warns of impending danger from buried high-power electric cables, in the yard or work site of your mark.

Solder

As any home handyfolk knows, there is rosin-core solder and there is acid-core solder. It is a huge no-no to use acid solder for any sort of delicate electrical connection as the acidic component will etch away the metal wiring. Getting some ideas?

C. F. Riggs suggests you buy a roll of each. Unwind the solder and exchange spools, putting the acid core solder back on the rosin spool. Then, deposit this roll of nasty solder on your mark's workbench if he or she does electrical repair or hobby work. If your mark happens to be the repairman of a store, you can probably drop off the roll quite easily, and just as easily drop off the mark's career.

Sources

Here is the master listing of places where you can find equipment, people, accessories and other items to make your Haydukery work. It is arranged in alphabetical order for your convenience.

Abbeon Cal, Inc. 123-285Y Gray Avenue, Santa Barbara, CA 93101
> Mark permanently with real paint pens and here's where you can get some. They wholesale the real thing in all colors.

Alcan Wholesalers, Inc. PO Box 2187, Bellingham, WA 98227
> Holy gung ho! These guys have a catalog crammed full of police, military and security goodies, equipment, chemicals and supplies. They're real.

Baron Samedi, Box 2084, Glenview, IL 60025
> This evil chap guarantees "voodoo revenge" on your enemies. Anywhere, anyone and fast. Guaranteed for only $25.

Baytronics, Box 591, Sandusky, OH 44870
> Vets especially will appreciate the huge stocks of GI surplus common equipment here, some of it very modern. They have all sorts of communication gear.

Blackhawk, Rt. 1, Box 221, Blue River, WI 53518
A chemical supply house that sells hard-to-find goodies by mail. When I last looked, chloroform was featured at two ounces for $5.

Break Wind Enterprises, Box 77, Mt. Ida, AR 71957
These people sell all sorts of fart-related gadgets, signs and bumper stickers. They're my kind of tasteful folks.

Bumper, PO Box 22791, Tampa, FL 33622
For create-your-own bumper stickers, here's a printing device. They say it's cheap and portable. Write to them for free details.

Cardinal Publishing, 2071 Emerson, Jacksonville, FL 32207
If you need blank certificates, here they are—birth, baptismal, marriage/divorce, wills, awards, diplomas, etc.

Chemistry, PO Box 1881, Murfreesboro, TN 37133
These guys advertise all sorts of useful chemical agents. You can order with safety.

CRB, Box 56, Commack, NY 11725
Hear the feds before they hear or find you! CRB sells books and equipment that reveal all the "secret" frequencies of the FBI, CIA, ATF, FCC, customs, and the military. This is like a big supermarket for buggers, antibuggers, and others who want to know who is listening to what and why.

Dwan Starks, 515 Byrne St., Petersburg, VA 23803

Learn the secrets of locksmithery (aka lockpicking), with books, instructions, tools, accessories and equipment. A starter kit is available for $5.

Ephemera, Inc. 275 Capp St., San Francisco, CA 94110

Perverted and disgusting buttons are the forte here, and they also do custom work. Bad taste is their hallmark.

Freedom Press, Box 2451, Farmington Hills, MI 48024

This place is like having access to a major library on chemical, biological and explosive warfare. They sell how-to books, plans and formulas to Haydukers everywhere. These are good folks.

Funny Side Up, 425 Stump Rd., North Wales, PA 19454

This is an adult version of the old Johnson Smith catalog. You need a copy of this class clown's bible.

Gims, Box 45212-452, Baton Rouge, LA 70816

Fill up your first-aid kit from this legitimate wholesale medical supply house, which sells medical treatment equipment and supplies. A catalog costs $5 (refundable with order).

Inkadinkado, Inc., 105 South St., Boston, MA 02111

Rubber stamps + your imagination = grand fun. These people furnish hundreds of splendid, creative and custom rubber stamps and accessories. The rest is up to your wonderful mind.

Kansas City Vaccine Co. PO Box 5713, Kansas City, MO 04102

These folks sell all pet products and drugs . . . real drugs. One item that may interest you is rabies vaccine.

Lindsay Publications, Inc. PO Box 12, Bradley, IL 60915

This is a very interesting publishing house, offering a lot of old-fashioned how-to books for the person who wants to be independent and self-reliant. There are all sorts of technical goodies available here and the catalog is free.

Male Order Photolabs, 18718 Ventura Blvd., Tarzana, CA 91356

This lab will process your sexually explicit photographs and get them back to you safely. The cost is $8.95 per twenty-four exposures, plus a buck for postage. They accept MC and VISA. They're O.K. merchants.

Mesa Books, Drawer 1798-AX, Denver, CO 80201

Choose from a list of more than five-dozen books loosely related to survival and nastiness to your enemies. The incredible price is just $1 per book . . . neat titles, too. Their motto is "Ban Defeat." I can get into that.

Norstarr, PO Box 5585, Pocatello, ID 83202

Make your own explosives and fireworks. They supply everything, including instructions, formulae and all ingredients for explosives, smoke dyes, etc. Catalog is $1.

Nova Detection Systems, 11684 Ventura Blvd, Studio City, CA 91604

Need a telephone line transmitter? They sell a kit that is a very dangerous threat to your mark's privacy.

Overthrow, PO Box 392, Canal Street Station, New York, NY 10013

The official newspaper of the Youth International Party (Yippies), this great publication contains more truth than many straight media. I've been a satisfied reader for years. It's worth the price of a subscription, well worth it.

PBS Livestock Drugs, 2800 Leemont Avenue, Canton, OH 44711

If your mark may be considered livestock, you will find PBS a sweet source of biologicals and other veterinary drugs and products. They have a $1 catalog with some disturbing implements and medicines for sale.

P & K Enterprises, Box 6155, Minneapolis, MN 55406

Their motto is "We print any message." And they do it on bumper stickers for a very reasonable price. Here's where you get those rotten personal bumper stickers printed for your mark's car.

P.W., 237 W. Houghton Lake Drive, Prudenville, MI 48651

Any message printed and no minimums for this bumper-sticker business. They sell 'em for two bucks each.

Seton Name Plate Corp., PO Drawer DF-1331, New Haven, CT 06505

This fine industrial firm has a huge catalog full of plastic and metal signs—identification products. These are stick-ons, bolt-ons, etc., and they look real because they are real.

Shotgun News, PO Box 669, Hastings, NB 68901

It's 100 percent advertising and the world's greatest single source of guns, knives, etc. This is the gun nut's bible. If it's destructive, someone will advertise it in *Shotgun News.*

SME, PO Box 251, Warren, OH 44482

Ohio must be the explosives center of the U.S. Here is yet another buckeye boomer offering all sorts of blow-em up goodies, smoke grenades, etc. Send SASE for custom specs and consulting, too.

Ron Smith Productions, 9000 Sunset Blvd., Hollywood, CA 90069

This is the man with more than 500 doubles and talented impressionists for the celebrities of yesterday and today.

Sooner Supply, Box 454, Lawton, OK 73502

A handyfolk's supply of chemicals, casings and other supplies to make fireworks. A catalog costs you a buck.

Trident, 2875 South Orleans, Milwaukee, WI 53227

This is a mail-order chemical house with lots of fun stuff at fair prices. Send your wants and SASE.

Walter Drake, The Drake Building, Colorado Springs, CO 80940

This is one of those little catalogs your mother

gets, full of cutesy gifts and novelty items for the house. It also is a Hayduker's delight . . . lots of custom-printed and specialty items useful for dealing with marks. It's one of my favorites.

WASP, PO Box 5091-AB, Steamboat Springs, CO 80477
Invest $5 in this catalog of discounted medical supplies and equipment. They sell all sorts of drugs, supplies, instruments and medicines at cheap prices.

The Wild Geese, Postfach 1145, 6460 Gelnhausen, Federal Republic of Germany
These folks do some publishing and some printing. They claim to be on the cutting edge of mercenarydom, but that may be a shill. Whatever, they offer some wonderful printing services, including death warrants, search warrants, interesting ID cards, etc.

YS & Company, PO Box 6713, Salinas, CA 93912
Give yourself an alibi with one of the taped, sound-effect cuts on this company's cassettes. Great background sounds to play in the background of your telephone calls. I have this product—it's very useful.

Zebra Mail Center, PO Box 11028, Houston, TX 77391
Your mail will be confidentially received, forwarded, remailed, held, or whatever else you wish. The Zebra motto is "use our address as your own." Free details.

Sports

At last, something to replace the old balm in the jock stunt so hoary to so many of us old sports from the scholastic locker-room wars. Yes, a tip of the old helmet to C. B. Gunslinger for this idea.

"I was the last guy out of the locker room after the morning practice one day last summer, because I wanted to get back at this football animal for some cheap hits he'd taken at me. I got his helmet off the top of his locker and pissed in it, making sure I basted the mouthpiece heavily.

"That afternoon, I was laughing so hard at the thought of this jerk thinking the moisture in his helmet and on his mouthpiece was caused by his own sweat that the coach gave me hell for not being serious enough. If he only knew . . ." says C. B. with another big roar of joviality.

The moral to this story, as all coaches like morals, is, "Don't get your teammates pissed off at you."

Stereos

From the storehouse of brotherly love we again welcome C. B. Gunslinger to transmit a tip on dealing with loud stereos. He notes that his brother and his punk friends inspired this idea.

"I need to study or want to be alone to read and my brother and his damn friends crank up the stereo and keep me awake until 3 a.m. It happened all too often," Gunslinger relates. "I stopped that nonsense. Every time he'd blare his stereo I'd just turn on my CB radio and key the mike a few times. It sends great shrill, piercing noises squealing through the stereo speakers."

Happiness means that the Gunslinger brothers have reached an agreement to please all concerned. C. B. says this cooperation concept will work for people in other apartments and houses, too.

Remember that old college game called "Switch," favored by Greeks, where you moved your thumb from location to location on command? Several readers noted the idea that switching components on stereo equipment might advance the cause of Haydukery. For example, switch capacitors and resistors, or solder bridges between previously unjoined points. Cut a wire at a junction, but leave it in place mechanically. All of this fun stuff will cost the mark lots of repair dollars.

Stink Bombs

Freshly soiled diapers make great close-quarter attack bombs, according to the Hombre of Justice. He says they work great in hot weather, especially if flung into the mark's face, food and/or drink at day's end or beginning. Have a nice day.

The formulae for other stink bombs, these delightful potions, continue to pour in. And since we really can't package Uncle Gerry's Expulsions into a practical delivery system, we'll have to make do with the next best devices. One of these came from Filthy McNasty and Vera.

"It's vile, disgusting and will make strong men weep. But it works and here's how," F & V write. "Take a small jar and break an egg into it. Stir well, then add an equal volume of urine straight from the tap. Mix well and leave uncapped for twenty-four hours. Then, cap it tightly and set aside for a month.

"After thirty days, hold your breath, open the jar and strain whatever comes out into another container. Apply as and where needed with mirth and guaranteed results."

If your mark has done anything to you that requires a fishy response, thank Tanya for the following. She says a small squid tossed somewhere into a very warm climate will putrify in a very short time and become a vile-smelling mess for a very long time.

She also relates that abalone will get totally sickening if put into a jar of water for a week and left in the sun for another week. The odor is "indescribable, but awful . . . don't get near it," she notes.

Studs

Our expolitico from New England wonders how it would look if your mark, a happily married man who'd been true to the little lady always and forever—even when they were first dating at Sam Jackass High School—were to get a "Happy Birthday Daddy" card from out of town with the name of another female high-school classmate on the return address? That's a long sentence, either way you cut it.

Success Stories

As I have so happily proved, Hayduking has become one of the world's finer participant sports. More people are commercializing on that fact. In Montgomery, Alabama, there's a firm known as Dirty Deeds and they specialize in what they advertise as "sweet revenge." For twenty-five dollars a shot they do such things as mail dead rats, push pies in the mark's face, deliver dead turkeys to local politicos and award "Bitch of the Year" plaques to . . . ?

According to owners Sherrie Campbell and Cathy Capp, a pair of former kindergarten teachers, they want to franchise the operation and go national. "All over America, people are dying to get even with other people," they claim.

Don't we know it, ladies. It all started right here. And, as Uncle George says with a knowing grin, "Lemmings must know something we don't."

The disciples of Hayduke remain active. There are rat-a-grams, dead flowers by mail or delivery, and I hear that George Hunter III of Leavittown, PA, is escalating the buffoonery. For forty-five dollars, Hunter gets nasty in a black costume, and white facial makeup, loads an old casket with ugly dead weeds and flowers, then delivers it to the person of your choice. "People in this country like to get back at other people. That's my market," Hunter claims.

True, amigo, just remember who started it all. The best news is that the classy practitioners are coming through with a veneer of professionalism that will raise Haydukery to a life form recognized along with the other classics, i.e., we might even make the Yellow Pages one of these days. The leading hitter in the pro ranks is Dick Smegma, action-able chief of the Revenge Squad. Dick is a prolific contributor to these pages and as his last year's yuletime greeting card set the tone: Merry Syphilis and a Clappy New Year!

Many years ago when I was still flying, I used to pilot for the local jump club. So did Palm Beach's Bob who told me a funny story about it. A friend of his flew an old DC-3 for local jump clubbers who used to make practical jokes a lot.

He got back at them by sneaking his copilot into the plane secretly before the jumpers loaded. The pilot came strolling in last and told the guys he was flying solo that day as the copilot was ill. They told him, "No sweat." He smiled as he closed the cabin door and prepared for takeoff.

About five minutes into the flight, the pilot locked the cabin door behind him as he strolled down the deck toward the open jump door. Unknown to the jumpers, the copilot was flying the ship.

"She's on auto pilot, guys, I guess, so have fun. . . ." the pilot shouted as he jumped out of the ship with his own parachute.

The rest of the plane emptied faster and cleaner than some of the trousers worn by the jump-team members.

Someone in Crown Point, Indiana, used a caulking gun and liquid nails to seal shut all 102 of the small town's parking meters, giving citizens a big break. Although police did charge a local carpenter, nobody said anything one way or the other about it. In the end, they had to let him go. No hard evidence.

Thanks to Jeff Woiton of Dallas, I learned

about a Hayduking that took place in the cold winter of 1985. Jeff set me a clip from the *Dallas Times Herald* explaining how some pranksters spilled ethyl mercaptan in the lobby of a fancy high-rise condo. The authorities thought it was a natural gas leak and ordered an evacuation.

Suitcases

How you handle this next nasty depends upon how subtle you want to be or how mean. According to Travel Agent Paco, my main man from Mexico, you simply stuff your mark's suitcase(s) with poison ivy. For maximum mental effect, leave the vines and leaves in the suitcase until the mark finds them. For maximum total physical effect, remove the ivy only after you have carefully crushed it and rubbed it all around the inside of the case, being certain that the nasty secretions from the plant go everywhere. Happy tripping, Mark!

Summer Camps

Time to put away the jokes about Jason, poison ivy and Camp Crystal Lake. I have a real question from a real contributor. He is Captain Video and he has served a tour of duty as a camp counselor for a bunch of ten- to sixteen-year-old kids, some of whom are really obnoxious little bastards. Let the captain explain.

"I have delightfully pulled some of your pranks on adults, but hesitate to pull them on kids. Maybe some of your other readers have also served as summer-camp counselors and would be kind enough to share some of the devilish and nasty things they did that were suitable for deserving little peckerheads."

Let's hear from present and former counselors.

Supermarkets

Filthy McNasty and lady Vera are back in the Hayduke news with some fine updates on supermarket revenge. Here's their first dispatch.

Either you or a friend go into the supermarket and buy a bottle of catsup, steak, barbeque or spaghetti sauce and take it home. Open it and insert several dead cockroaches, beetles, dead lizards, or whatever. Reseal the bottle or jar and return it, saying that you got the wrong brand, and exchange it, without letting the clerk look into the bottle. Some supermarket geek will put it back on the shelf. Eventually, some customer will buy it, and come dinner time. . . . Back it goes with a full-blown case of hysteria, let's hope right in front of other shoppers.

For another stunt, walk into the market with a friend or two, making sure you are well within earshot of as many customers as possible. Discuss the recent outbreak of botulism poisoning that the health department has traced to that particular market. This is especially good if the market has a deli or hot food take-out service.

Still talking, even though the Tylenol cyanide poisonings are old hat now, mention how the police are looking for a copycat poisoner in the area of the market of your choice. You can add a twist to this also. As you are in the checkout line with a few groceries, start eating from a bag of potato chips, cookies, or whatever that you are buying. Be sure that lots of customers can see you.

Suddenly clutch your chest, then your stomach, and act as if you are poisoned. Make disgusting noises, and generally give the impression that you are going to croak right there in the market. Scream that the stuff you were eating was poisoned. A couple of accomplices whisk you out of the store into a car to "go to the hospital emergency room." You make a clean getaway. Improvise on this one and you can have a lot of fun.

It's great to have my buddies back—the terror of the supermarket cabal—Filthy McNasty and Vera. Not only are they fun folks, but they concoct, perform and write well about funny things. This time, they are taking an even bigger dump on the supermarkets. What set off this terrific tirade by this terrible twosome? The daughter of a good friend was a stockperson at a local produce pit and was the victim of extreme sexual abuse, economic butchery and employer violence, compounded by the old-boy network of the local newspaper, small-town officials, the courthouse crowd, etc. You recognize the usual cesspool of small-town crap. Enter Filthy and Vera.

Filthy said he first set himself up as a bag boy at the mark's huge emporium of grocery grossness. It was easy. He just copped a white apron, dressed as they dress and became a four-dollar an hour moron carrying out folks' grocery bags. Let Filthy pick up the story.

"After bagging a customer to the car, round up five or six empty carts and look for a customer just entering or leaving their cage [biker lingo for a car]. Choose an expensive set of wheels or look for people who appear to be uptight creeps.

"Then roll that thundering row of carts broadside into their car . . . whammmm, you know what that does to cheap car doors. The people will bitch and yell. Tell them to bitch at the owner, the carts are his, not yours. When they persist, tell them to screw off. When they steam off to the store, you split."

You might come back to the same place a week or so later and repeat this same stunt.

Filthy and Vera's second chapter involves you and/or your surrogate bag boys standing outside the store or just inside the door offering straight customers some new premiums for shopping there. Offer them acid, a joint, some hash, a swig of scotch from your bottle, some kiddy porn, maybe even flash someone. *Be prepared to make a fast exit on this one,* so control your laughter. It's tough to run when you're hysterical.

Filthy and Vera say this next one takes balls, but I think it mostly takes good, strong arms and fast feet. They call it "Food fight" and it becomes obvious as you read.

A bunch of friends, six to ten, go casually into the mark's store. After a minute or so for all to get settled into a location (preplanning is vital here), the leader grabs one of those PA system phones for in-store announcements and says "Attention shoppers. (Mr./Ms. mark's name), our manager, welcomes you to our seventh annual food fight. Participate and win a $200 gift certificate and, remember, it's all legal and all in fun."

With that, your shills start flinging everything they can at each other and at the straight customers, who, hopefully, will join in. Try to throw stuff that makes splashy messes.

Tip over people's carts, pie them, spill food from shelves, fire spray cans of shaving cream and whipped cream at people as you dash by. Totally trash the place. Obviously, you and your ringleaders will wish to escape before order is restored and blame begins to settle out of the messy chaos. You have about ten minutes on this stunt. Who says market day has to be boring!

Are we having fun, gang? You bet!!!

Let's tone down the levity for a moment and do something very subtle, simple and effective. Locate the mark store's silent alarm—they all have them. Set it off or short it out. Split fast, or just continue to shop if you were able to hit the alarm without being spotted (watch for TV cameras and surveillance mirrors).

Or, here's another stunt. Most markets have outdoor banners and signs with the weekly specials advertised. Some creative editing will alter "Ground Beef 89¢ Per Pound," or whatever the store has, to "Fresh Dog Crap 49¢ a Pound," or "Fermented Iranian Pimples 15¢ Ea," or "Fresh Wino Piss, $1 a Pint."

Speaking of whom, do you know some old winos? You can probably bribe several of them to lie down in front of the mark's market and drink their bottles. It may repel a few customers. Also, bribe one of the winos to puke on someone.

Sweeties

My old pal LTC MAC is a devoted reader of *Easy Riders* and other literature of the genre. A gentle, Christian man and former Sunday School teacher, LTC Mac shares his fine way of bringing some new friends into your former sweetie's life if she has proved to you that this is what she desires.

Write some very simple, friendly letters in her name to folks incarcerated in the nation's prisons. All sorts of cons write letters to *Easy Riders, Overthrow, The la Free Press,* etc., requesting pen pals and more. LTC MAC wants only to help everyone achieve maximum karma.

He suggests that you not make the letters too friendly or they will appear phony. As he notes, the idea is to entice the con to write back, hoping he/she will be one of the nastier ones who use these ads to bait unsuspecting marks themselves. It isn't too hard to figure this out when you read some of the magazines. Try to avoid obviously sincere cons as a lot of them are in prison in America and do not belong there, just as a lot of people at the top of government and industry belong in the very worst prisons we can find.

Among the things you can offer the cons in your "Sweetie's" letter are jobs, money, more letters, help with parole, visits, smuggling, and sexy photos. Be sure to include a sexy—but not gross—photo with a second letter. Second letter? Sure, write again as the real sweetie will probably ignore the con's first response letter. It doesn't matter whose picture you send, by the way.

Elmer Groin's girlfriend was given the shaft by so many other guys that her mother, a prudish divorcée, nagged the hell out of Elmer to marry this girl. Elmer, a computer engineer, was a nice, rich nerd. But he wasn't dumb without a sense of deviousness.

"I set up a loud, boastful jerk at work with my soon-to-be exgirlfriend, without telling her. I showed him her picture and said what a great and easy lay she was. Half of that was true, anyway," Elmer related.

Now, comes the kicker. Elmer gave the guy the address of the girl's mother's apartment and let him in with a key he had "borrowed" about ten minutes before mother was due home from work. He told the guy to get undressed and to surprise the lady, as she got all hot when surprised like that.

At this point, dear reader, I'll close the page on this true story so you might fantasize the climax with your own creative imagination.

My friendly New Jersey woodcutter, Mr. Justice, has a fun idea for revenge involving a straying lady, although it would also work with a husband. Here is Mr. Justice's idea.

Recruit a trusted female friend to phone the mark's husband and say, "Keep your wife away from my husband." Let's proceed with the heterosexual scenario. The accomplice continues, "He swore the affair was over last year, but I have proof they are at it again. Just keep your whoring wife away from my man . . ." Stop and break into a brief bit of semi-hysteria here.

Continuing, the accomplice also says there are photos of the couple and that she will share them when she gets them back from the lab. When the mark cries out, "Who is this?" The accomplice says, "I'm sure you know . . . just tell your slut wife to stay away from my man." Then she hangs up.

Everyone likes to receive mail. So leave it to me to create an exception. If you have an exsweetie who's done you rotten, go to your favorite tabloid publication that features classified personals of a very intimate, personal nature. Look for an ad that offers to exchange pictures and intimate dialogue. Compose a letter from your exsweetie, getting a friend of whatever sex to help you with the handwriting. Be inventive and very explicit. Remember, you're writing a sales letter, i.e., soliciting. Be sure to include a snappy photo of your ex or someone who's really sexy looking.

The following happened to a reader of mine. He gave his girlfriend money toward buying her own car, bought her a ring, lots of clothes, stocked her pantry and sprang for dinner at good restaurants at least twice a week. Her response was to hang out in bars on his two work nights a week and let herself get picked up by local college kids, although she swore they never went to bed.

He decided that since he couldn't marry her he would help her have the wedding anyway. A printer did invitations, our hero placed the story in the local paper complete with announcement photo of the bride. The caterer was ordered and all was set for the date. The surrogate groom? It was an old drunk scarffed up from a local gin mill who was paid $100 for the stunt.

Everything clicked in place. The story/picture of the bride ran in the local paper Friday and all the usual wedding stuff happened Saturday, including the "groom" who showed up at both the church and at "his" bride's home. Naturally, everything and everyone there was in a total turmoil. To add to the fun, the "groom" was drunk as could be.

The bride had no idea what was happening. Curious friends were calling, the church was calling, the caterer had arrived and there was a smelly old wino at the door insisting he was marrying the young lady of the house.

"Best wedding I ever planned," chuckled our triumphant reader.

Here is an unusual, but not rare situation. Your friend's sweetie has just done a number on him or her. For whatever reason you are among the emotional casualties. From previous books you know all the SOP fight-backs. Here's a little deeper tactic from Chester the Spoon, a master of dish-it-out deviousness.

"When a couple breaks up, the dumpee is probably slandering the dumper all over the place. If you, the friend, got hurt, too, keep on the pressure. It ain't nice, but, keep reminding your friend how rotten the other party is and what wildly sexual thing the other party is likely doing now with everyone and anyone. Nasty, yes, but it will keep the pressure and the flow of rotten tricks on the ultimate target," says Chester.

Little Tommie Titmouse didn't get angry when his sweet young lady was a mite unfaithful. Indeed, this gentleman even offered to help her broaden her services. He ambled on down to his favorite printer and got a couple hundred index-sized business cards printed that advertised—using her name—"Sweetie's Unusually Erotic Massages." He also included her parents' telephone number as she lived at home, her hours of noon until 3 a.m., one price for all, and no tipping. He also put the Visa and MasterCard logos in the upper borders of the card.

The cards were posted in bars, motels, phone booths, the local airport and bus station and in the day rooms of the local military base. If your exsweetie lives alone, Tommie says you should print the girl's at-work number.

Tanya from Long Beach is one mean

Hayduker. Here goes.

"I used the gentian or methyl violet stunt on a little tease who came on to my husband during a week-long camping trip, but only after she finally embarrassed me publicly. I got even privately.

"I put it into a box of expensive and intimate dusting powder, wrapped it in fancy paper and sent it to her. Inside I included a typed personal card telling her this was a sample of a new product from a local ritzy store. She should enjoy it while she looked over the credit-card applications, which I also enclosed as a part of the cover."

Tanya reports that friends told her this young tease's boyfriend wore a long, unhappy face for a long time, which means the stunt struck home.

Tar

I'll never forget the expression on the face of Raymundo Diáz when he told me, "The man with access to a bucket of tar has more power than the man with an eighteen-inch neck in a barroom fight." As always, Ray's priorities are on schedule.

It takes less time for me to tell you to obtain a bucket of roofing tar from your nearest lumber yard than it does for you to think of ways to use this natural weapon against your mark. Consider the thick, gooey nature of this substance and how it adheres to almost everything with the same serious tenacity. Need references? Ask your mother, spouse or anyone else who has had the unsuccessful frustration of attempted tar removal from objects like clothing, car interiors, skin, hair, food, lawns, gardens, pets, children, paintings, water systems, air conditioners, and so on and on and on.

Tar belongs, Haydukers. Enjoy its immoderate use.

Tattoos

Tattoo fun can be contagious, as I realized when my friend Don the Registrar showed up with one on his shoulder. He told me he got loaded beyond control and just had it done. That got me to planning.

Suppose you had a really mean mark who was straight in all ways except with booze. He was a mean drunk. After you got him loaded, a custom tattoo artist could come to the safehouse location and put just about anything your cash would buy on that resting mark. Dozens of fresh tattoo ideas are rushing into my mind as I create this sentence, spilling over each other to be first in line to mess up this mark's future with his world. Do you have any idea of the impression given by a large, gross tattoo on someone's forehead?

Taxidermy

It's a fun time when Uncle George leaves his Idaho redoubt and rolls his customized Zapata mobile home in for a visit at Ft. Hayduke. It means evenings of fun, drink, love 'n laughter as we rerun, over and over, the memories of our silly youth. This last time, Uncle George had an idea to quell the curious and, as he put it, "to piss off nearly everyone, as I've finally found the universal disgust switch."

Uncle George says to locate a previously living puppy or small dog, first choice being a cocker spaniel. Your actual choice would depend upon you, your territory, neighbors, friends, and related factors. Your next choice is that of finding a taxidermist to mount the head and paws properly.

"Raw, disgusted shock is what you're going for," Uncle George roared as he explained this to me. "If you're lucky, they'll think you killed it, and with imagination you can come up with a suitably distasteful war story of slow, painful mayhem."

Nurture this one well, gentle reader.

Teachers

A lot of us owe where and what we are in life to our teachers. That thought alone must piss off a whole lot of folks daily, including their teachers. Want to have some fun with the teachers anyway? Some teachers like to be really unresponsive to legitimate questions, during exams, for example. Chester the Spoon says you can crack this facade by either noisily throwing up and/or fainting during the exam period. A faked seizure also works, as I have found out through some nefarious experience of my own.

When he wrote to me, Mark Fedyk was a nice kid, a bright, high-school senior. Somehow, I feel that Nelson Chunder's book matured him. Anyway, he pulled off a grand stunt and now that the statute of limitations has expired, i.e., he has been graduated, we can share this with you for your own use or enjoyment.

He worked in the school print shop where they produced complaint cards for teachers to use to communicate with the principal which students had been naughty. Mark made up a card for a fictitious student named "Mike Hunt" and slipped it in with some real ones.

After some time hunting through records for this mysterious student and finding nothing, the principal of this large school thought it must be a new student or a transfer and that the paperwork had not yet caught up with him. So he asked his secretary to page the student on the school's general PA system which went into every room during the morning homeroom period. She did.

"Would Mike Hunt please report to the principal's office immediately."

Mark says the laughter could be heard for blocks.

Telephone Solicitors

At long last, a ringy dingy way to handle rude, nasty and unwanted telephone solicitations. Thanks to Lancelot A. Barward and Karen Feldman Smith of Ft. Myers, Florida, for sharing the way. And here it is.

Sam Sewell, a Ft. Myers resident, has dedicated himself to driving these intrusive telephone solicitors from Florida. As part of his battle, he listens to the solicitation long enough to learn what company is behind it and their address. Then, he bills them for his time. The following is the form of letter Sam uses.

August 16, 1985

Dear telephone solicitor and electronic trespasser:

This is to advise you that on _____ at _____ your representative _____ used our leased phone line and our telephone equipment. We lease a phone line and purchase equipment to serve our needs. We do not want to be called by businesses at inconvenient times with unwelcome propositions. Accordingly, you are hereby assessed on a $ _____ line and equipment-access fee for use of our phone. An additional fee will be charged for all additional calls.

Please remit promptly to Sam Sewell, Ft. Myers, FL.

Failure to remit promptly will result in action in small-claims court to establish the right of a citizen to charge access fees to businesses who use a citizen's leased and owned

183

property. This is a well-established legal principle and by applying it to telephone solicitors we may be able to rid the state of Florida of a pestilence of epidemic proportions.

Access fee schedule:
Normal business hours $5
Outside business hours $10
Weekends $20

Sincerely,

Sam Sewell
(address)

In another life, Carla Savage was a starving student who had to work as a phone jockey to pay her bills. She gives the other side of the telephone solicitation business, with disabled vets, blind and other handicapped folks, struggling to make a buck. Her thought: please use an extra margin of care before you come down on these people indiscriminately.

But, when you do . . .

Carla says they all work on a commission basis. "If you order eighteen magazine subscriptions on Tuesday, they get their commission on Friday. If you cancel the order the next week or refuse to pay or whatever, that commission is then deducted from the next week's check."

They also get hell from the boss if this happens more than a set amount of times, like twice in a month. Neither of us had ever heard of any company taking a customer to court over small-ticket telephone solicitation, as all there has been is a verbal agreement over the telephone. Big-ticket items require a follow-up letter with formal agreement.

Here's how Carla handles the bad guys. Remember, she used to work this game, so pay attention. "When the caller is really obnoxious or calls at an ungodly hour, I make sure I get the name of the caller, the company and the telephone number, then listen until I get bored. I hang up and wait half an hour.

"I then call back and scream at whomever answers to talk to a supervisor *right now!* I usually get one. I explain, doing my best to sound the part of an hysterical middle-class housewife, that some sicko from this company has been calling my ten-year-old son/daughter with a sales pitch for a book or video tape on the delights of oral sex, or sodomy with farm animals, or something like that.

"I threaten with everything a housewife could think of, saying that my husband is a lawyer, or some sort of police authority, and will get them when he gets home, blah, blah, blah . . .

"By this time, the manager will probably ask me who made the call. You give him/her the name of the rude solicitor who started all of this with that inopportune telephone call. Naturally, you never give the manager your real name. Use the name of some secondary mark."

Another of Carla's fun ways to beat down obnoxious solicitors is to freelance for them, without their knowing it. If you're bored and have access to another private telephone, not your own, start calling people—either at random or as secondary marks. Identify yourself with some sleazy name, or the name of a tertiary mark, and say that you represent the solicitation company that you want to burn.

What do you sell? Carla says you can sell dildos in decorator or racial colors. Or sell kiddy porn. Sell drugs. Sell snuff films. But have fun by offending people in the name of this telephone solicitation firm you dislike.

Another former telephone solicitor, Welty Buttface, recalls doing this stunt several times and getting back at various marks each time. He often used a hoary old vaudeville joke that goes back to the WWI days of Sgt. Jim Kensinger and his Merry Bandsmen. "If you know who you are calling and depending on the gender of the one who answers, you ask, 'Do you have any explicit, nude photos of your (choose one or more) wife, husband, son, daughter, father, mother, etc.?'

"Believe it or not, unless the other person is really sharp, 95 out of 100 will answer with a shocked 'No.' So you ask them if they want to buy some, and then launch into a disgusting description of the photos."

Welty says he rarely got beyond the fourth or fifth sentence before the mark hung up. The law calls this either electronic harassment or terroristic threat by telephone means. This proves they have no sense of humor whatever and should be treated as such at all times.

Another scheme of Carla's is to burn up the salesperson's time and phone line. Ask a lot of questions, put the salesperson on hold "while you take another call," ask personal questions, ask advice. But also do your best to imitate a truly good customer. Make a real crisis over color choice on some $100 order. Chances are, Carla says, the salesperson will hang up on you. Call back and get the supervisor on the line, then report the salesperson for being rude and for hanging up on you while you were contemplating an order.

Telephones

This scam may have already disappeared as Ma Bell's Computer Police move in to destroy amateur phone freaks. But, as you'll be using pay telephones, it might be worth a try.

You want to call a good friend and talk for awhile. Send that friend a letter setting a specific date and very specific time when your friend will be at a pay telephone. You already have that telephone number. Or, you can reverse the roles.

Using fake names, place your call as a person-to-person collect call, making it to the pay telephone number. The best time to try this is early evening or on Sunday when the operators are busy. If you hear unusual sounds, clicks, or the words "coin check" from another voice, hang up and clear out fast.

You can help turn Ma Bell into an even meaner mother, though, at the expense of jerking your mark's long-distance trunk lines around. Muffle your voice a bit, and place a collect call to the mark from some safe, out of the way, pay telephone. Say the call is from (choose one) mom, dad, the kids, etc. It's better if you know actual names and that the "person" doing the calling is out of town. It's much better to have the call made from way far away so it adds more to the mark's bill. When he or she accepts the call, try to keep the mark on the line as long as possible. All sorts of funny and creative planning could go into that aspect of this stunt.

Despite advertising to the contrary, the "new"

cordless telephones are not really all that secure from outside ears. One expert, Jimmy Carter, tells us that even cheap ham-radio receivers can pick up transmissions from these telephones. You can listen, record and otherwise use your mark's cordless telephone conversations to your advantage if you're in range, can find the frequency and know how to use this illegally obtained information. I'll leave that part of it to you recreational hamsters who enjoy electronic sleuthery.

If you have access to your mark's telephone when it rings and are lucky enough to have a telephone solicitor on the line, by all means go for it. This bit of advice came from Charlie Porker, who used to run a boiler room of phone banks for national political candidates.

"Most of these numbers are dialed automatically, so the sales jockey already has the called name and number on his display screen. Keep that in mind so you don't try to order stuff for your mark from your own phone if the sales person calls on your own line," he advises.

"Hopefully, the solicitation will be for something the mark has absolutely no use for. Try to keep the order under $100, as a larger amount is usually verified."

This idea can be modfied for an office where it is easy to use extension telephones and not so easy to check on who has ordered what for whom. Here is where you can use someone else's telephone to make outgoing calls ordering several gross of imprinted pens, key chains, T-shirts, etc. Naturally, sales companies will insist that custom-printed items be paid for, which will continue to create fun for the mark long after the packages have arrived. But, remember, heed Charlie's advice . . . don't get greedy. Keep the order routine and on the modest side.

The Ten Commandments of Revenge

And now, thanks to the Apostle of Revenge, Dick Smegma, I humbly present for your perusal, belief and adherence, the Ten Commandments of Revenge. Stay faithful and you'll have a lot of yucks without the heartbreak of being caught.

1. Thou shalt not trust, nor confide in, anyone!
If you do, that person could eventually betray you. Even if it is a relative or spouse, don't tell them what you are up to. Implicated accomplices are OK.

2. Thou shalt never use thine own telephone for revenge business!
Always use a public telephone, or an unwitting mark's, so calls cannot be traced back to you, or someone who knows you.

3. Thou shalt not touch revenge documents with thy bare hands!
Bare hands leave fingerprints! Wear gloves.

4. Thou shalt become a garbage collector!
Once your victim places his garbage outside his home/office for pickup, it is 100 percent legal for you to pick it up yourself. You can learn about your victim by sifting through his trash. The pros do it all the time.

5. Thou shalt bide thy time before activating a revenge plot!

Give the victim time to forget about you and what he has done to wrong you. Getting even too quickly makes it easier for him to discover *who* is doing it!

6. Thou shalt secure a "mail drop" address in another city!

You don't want revenge mail being traced back to your residence/town, do you?

7. Thou shalt learn everything there is to learn about thy victim!

The best revenge schemes/plans are hatched by people who know their victim *better* than their victim does.

8. Thou shalt pay cash all the time in a revenge plot!

Checks, money orders, etc., can be traced back to you. Cash cannot!

9. Thou shalt trade with merchants who have never heard of you!

Do business with people only *once* when involved in a revenge plot. Possibly wear a disguise so they will have trouble identifying you in a legal confrontation.

10. Thou shalt never threaten thy intended victim!

Why warn your intended victim that you are going to get even? When bad things begin to happen to your victim, whether or not you caused them, your victim will remember your threat, and *he'll* set out to even the score with you.

Theaters

Are you bothered by tall people sitting in front of you at concerts or films? Here is an easy cure. Either bring to the theater or fill in the theater restroom, a twelve- to sixteen-ounce container of water. Pour it slowly on the seat in front of you. Nobody will want to stay in a wet seat. Caution: You might warn people before they sit down in front of you that others tried to sit there earlier, but the seat(s) is(are) wet.

If you hate the theater, having cause to get back at the management, substitute some kind of glue, rubber cement, corn syrup, or something else gooey for water. Again, be kind, warn the potential sitters first. If it's your lucky day, maybe they will be obnoxious jerks who will tell you to mind your own business and sit down anyway.

Tires

The Greasy Mechanic suggests that if you want to hurt your mark in his/her ride that you pay attention to the tires. New radial tires are designed to roll in only one direction. So, switch sides and get the tires running in the opposite direction. As Mark Hastings adds, "This action will make the tires squirm and shimmy worse than a hyperactive four-year-old at a long wedding."

Toilet Tissue

Oliver Snot is one of the cleanest people I know. He is also one of the most frugal. That's why he tries to recycle everything, including nose-blown tissues.

"I dry it and refold it so someone else can use it again," Oliver says. "If I don't like the next user, I try to fold it with the big boogers and lungers still in there, when I replace the tissue in the mark's container."

Can you imagine recycled tissue paper being really desirable for use? If so, how do you feel about previously used toilet paper?

Toilets

There must be a lot of cement merchants and plumbers in cahoots in our great nation. During talk shows and in my mail bag, I have about a dozen accounts of cementing a toilet. Here's a summary.

Turn off the water supply to the toilet, flush it, then flush once more. The tank or bowl will not refill, obviously. Fill up the bowl with wet cement and trowel it level before you close the lid. As an added sentiment, you might use your finger to spell some rude, scatalogical message to your mark.

Travel

A lot of my domestic travel time is in those areas of the country where cops play speed trap with crooked technology and old boy magistrates. That's why I enjoyed hearing Gary's story about adding an aluminum storage tank and electric pump in the trunk of his souped-up car, along with a hose aimed out the back.

"I filled the tank system with sulphur dioxide. Then I got the old bully boy fuzz on my tail in his pathetic Dodge patrol car and led him out of town in a mini-chase. I opened up on him at about fifty feet and engulfed him in this cloud of foggy gas. He ran clear off the road and dumped his car ass-end into a swamp."

This gas burns and chokes a person, obviously messing up his vision. Gary said he picked an area where no real harm could come to the officer and fired his blast before they got up to any unsafe speed.

Of course, as Richard Stone points out so cogently, "Where there is no patrol car there is no speed limit."

Moving from the highway to one of the great travelers of the world, the late LuLu McManmon, sister of mighty Bruno, used to say "if you're going to travel on the Titanic you might as well go first class." She had this great idea for motels, tour-ship staterooms and other habitats of the ill-treated tourist. She used to do this to expensive dumps that went out of their way to make her stay miserable.

"I always think positively so I thought misery might like company," LuLu told me once. "You know how these places store extra soap and towels in the closet? I used to carefully unwrap the soap, stick a bunch of my tight 'n curlies [aka pubic hairs] on the soap, wrap it back up and replace it in storage for the next guest."

Yeah, LuLu, I bet that made a big hit with the management when the next guest called to raise hell about the short hairs on the soap.

More hijinks from the Skull, only this time the fun happens before the mark gets off the ground. Skull says to make a piece of metal or foil into the shape of a gun or nasty looking dagger and then slip it into your mark's carry-on airline luggage.

"This really works well because the piece of metal or foil is really thin," says Skull. "You can put it between folded clothes in a briefcase between photographs or pages in a book. There are dozens of hiding places where it will not be easily found, except by the airport metal detector or X-ray machine."

Always be on the lookout for double fun by also sticking a very small plastic bag of white powder in the mark's bag or pocket.

TV Sets

There is an afterlife for the older cordless telephones so thoughtlessly assigned to the dump by the planned obsolescence of Japanese technology and American marketing. According to Lindley Cajones, these older models, generally pre-1983 units, really mess up TV reception within 500 to 600 feet of being used. Think about that . . . a portable TV thumper right there in your hand.

Typewriters

I have associates within the FBI who tell me to be careful of using your own typewriter for doing nasty mail using other people's names and addresses. Despite a lot of screw-ups in the FBI, their lab folks are sharp and can pretty well ID individual machines among mass-production runs of IBM typewriters.

The answer is either to use a coin typewriter from a public library in another town, as I suggested in my first book, or to rent one from an office equipment store. Buy your own typing ball from another store and use it on the rental. Replace the rental ball when you take the machine back. "To be warned is to be wise," and this comes from the FBI.

By the way, I assume you've watched enough detective shows on TV to know to use rubber gloves when handling paper and envelopes that are going to a mark. You just can't be too careful about fingerprints these days.

Underarms

There are many unfortunates who suffer from chronic underarm radiance, or as it's known in better clinics, armpit stench A sensitive person has only to shop among the huddled masses at any less than urban mall or supermarket on a weekend to appreciate this offense.

I propose a solution.

If your mark is one who suffers from this problem, a few gentle hints from an interested other party (spouse, friend, business associate, etc.) to use a powder deodorant will set up the next stage. Before going on, let's toss a hearty thanks to the ankle biters of Aunt Nancy's Nursery School for the remainder of this olfactory operation.

When the mark has been set up to the point of using the deodorant powder on a regular basis, you replace the top layer of that nice, gentle odor suppressant with 1) yeast powder, 2) wallpaper paste, 3) or something else along those same tacky lines.

Actually, it's an idea fit for a Brut.

Unwashed

You've worked with or shopped near someone who hasn't been near bathwater and soap for a week. In France, of course, it's their way of life. But, in a civilized country that is just not done. Rick from Denver has a suggestion.

"This guy at work rarely bathed. Seriously, you could not stand to be within five feet of him for very long. He stunk. No amount of subtle hinting worked," Rick relates.

"I bought a piece of raw chicken at the store and taped it under his desk out of the way. The other three of us in the office acted like nothing was wrong and went about our business.

"He must have found it over the weekend, because it was gone Monday and so was his own odor. We never had any problem after that."

Utilities

You've no doubt heard the expression, "Hold your water." Mark Hastings, a POW in Yuppieland, cements this pledge with good old-fashioned fervor. In his neighborhood, the water meters and shut-off valves are located out from the homes at the edge of the road. The controls are covered with metal lids and are in holes a foot or so deep.

Mark needed to pay back a nasty neighbor who had violated his rights and property and had the money to get away with it. Mark bought 160 pounds of concrete mix for $6.20. He shut off the neighbor's water valve, then filled the hole with the 160 pounds of quick-drying concrete one night.

"You would not believe the size of the hole the utility company had to dig in this guy's lawn to get his water service restored. The crew foreman gave *him* hell and the company billed *him* for the work," Mark reports.

Venereal Disease

Choose the sex of your caller carefully, but our old friend Bullet the Hemorrhoid says to call a local VD hotline or other health clinic and in really coy fashion explain that you think you've infected (mark's name) with a (be specific) strain of venereal disease. The name you use to report will not be important unless you make it too silly for credibility. Don't. You want the authorities to contact your mark.

Video

Did you ever want to make a "snuff film"? These movies or videos are really sick fantasies in which one or more of the stars is murdered, supposedly for real, usually while in the midst of or directly after some sexual act. In all my worldly travels and those of my associates, I have never seen any such films/videos outside of the news shown on television. Snuff films are just carefully done staging . . . fake all the way.

But that doesn't mean you can't do it, sort of.

Some *very* trusted friends who have experience with the video industry could help you. But I cannot stress the word "trust" enough. The idea is to make a tape using an actor or actress who is a dead ringer for your mark. The scenario from there is up to you:

- Mark as snuffer
- Mark as snuffee
- Mark as director/financier of snuff.

Another twist is to make a really scuzzy porno film with an actor/actress that looks like your mark.

Wine

The husband had spent twenty years painstakingly assembling one of the finest wine cellars in the Midwest. After six nasty months of divorce proceedings, the wife ended up owning the house and everything in it. The first time she went downstairs to fetch a bottle of '59 Lafite-Rothschild, she discovered that the labels had been soaked off every bottle, the lead foil peeled from every cork and all the bottles mixed up so that no two identical ones were in the same rack.

Women Beaters

I agree with Carla Savage that these scumbag beasts are right on the top of the list with child molesters when it comes time to hit back. But for this generic nastiness, according to Carla, your mark in this matter really doesn't have to be a full-time wife beater, any deserving jerk will do.

"Call the local shelter for battered women, usually late on a Friday or Saturday night as those seem to be prime hours when these creeps have to reassert their flagging masculinity by having a bunch of drinks and then knocking the old lady around," Carla says.

"Have a male friend do the talking. Have him sound a bit drunk, very surly and very foul-mouthed. Ask for the mark's wife or girlfriend by name. Mention the mark's name a lot, too, as it is 'him' making the call.

"Insist the attendant is lying if he or she tells you that the woman is not there or refuses to give out any information. That's SOP. Tell the attendant to put her on the phone or you'll come down there and forcefully take her home your own way.

"Get really nasty. Get sexist beyond the lunatic fringe. Threaten to torch the place. Threaten to rape everyone there. Make lesbian charges. Laugh when the attendant says he/she will call the police. Tell them you have an axe and explosives. Get angry and loud. Keep mentioning the mark's name and that of his wife or girlfriend.

Suddenly hang up."

Carla says to wait about fifteen minutes and have your friend call back. Have your friend sound all sweetness and light. He can't apologize enough. Have him cry a little. She says these jerks run in patterns like this. The idea is to make a very realistic performance. Accept the telephone counseling for a few minutes, then gradually get a bit more militant about a man's rights and that "even if you love (her name) a lot, she lies, etc." Build into that insulting, threatening rage again.

If your male friend is a good enough actor and you do a bit of research beforehand, Carla bets you can have the police at the mark's home with his second call outburst. Most shelters tape their calls, so keep that in mind, regarding what your male friend says and who your male friend is, i.e., pick someone who is not from the area.

Carla had to use this stunt on one of her exboyfriends who liked to beat up girls. She said it worked all the way, as outlined. She later found out the boyfriend spent a little time in the slam before his true alibi stood up. But you can bet your last dollar that the cops kept his name on a list. I know cops.

As a final comment, Carla asks that you save this plan for a last-ditch effort unless your local shelter has several telephone lines or uses volunteers with phone-forwarding services. She says, "Don't tie up their phone lines so that a truly legitimate emergency can't get through. Treat these numbers with the same respect you would 911."

Zippers

Chester the Spoon claims that liquid solder really messes up zippers. This tidbit of information is useful whether or not the mark is wearing clothing. This knowledge could be applied as well to a closed tent, imprisoning the campers. There are all sorts of uses for this plan. Thanks, Chester. Keep a zip upper lip!

Zowie, The Last Word

You should always have the last word, as long as I am guaranteed the last action. I would like to do another book and if you have any ideas, suggestions, stunts or tricks to share, please write and tell me all about them. Write to George Hayduke, PO Box 1307, Boulder, CO 80306. If you include a return address, I will write back personally. Also, please let me know what pen name you want me to use if I include your stunt in the next book, or, if you wish, I can use your real name. I don't know about you, but this stuff is true fun for me, so let's share the laughs. Write. Please? Or else!

AN UNUSUAL REQUEST

We've had curry, soups, ceremonies, mail order and sexual stunts involving roadkill. I guess a book is not out of the question. There is a graduate student named Dementia Dermaptera who is doing a book of roadkill photos.

"I ask your readers to take their cameras on the roadways of our world and photograph the roadkill. Then, send the photos to me and I will make a book of these photos. Each photographer will be credited with his pictured roadkill and the book will be published. I see this as a unique research effort," says Dermaptera.

Send your roadkill photos to: Dementia Dermaptera, PO Box 1307, Boulder, CO 80306. This coffee-table book will be out in better shops everywhere, soon.